STEPPING INTO MISSIONS

STEPPING INTO MISSIONS

A guided tour into what could be the rest of your life

Advantage
BOOKS

Jesse Mattix & Peggy Covert

Published by: ADVANTAGE BOOKS™
                  Longwood, FL
                  www.advbookstore.com

Library of Congress Catalog Number: 2021936307

Names: Mattix, Jesse, Author Covert, Peggy, Author

Title: Stepping into Missions: A guided tour into what could be the rest of your life / Jesse Mattix and Peggy Covert

Description   Longwood: Advantage Books, 2021

Identifiers: ISBN (print): 9781597556316, (mobi, epub): 9781597556439, Subjects: Missions

First Printing: April 2021
21 22 23 24 25 26   10 9 8 7 6 5 4 3 2 1

Table of Contents

Introduction

When we visited Jesse and his family in Peru they took us on an outing that included a picnic in a picturesque bamboo hut overlooking a gentle creek and surrounded by jungle vegetation. After the meal they suggested that we should walk up a trail to see a beautiful waterfall. Strangely enough, they didn't offer to go with us. The trail turned out to be more difficult than we expected and we never would have arrived at the waterfall without the help of a couple of local men who were upgrading the trail. One of them helped me down several steep, muddy slopes, and the other rearranged some rocks in the creek so we could cross without getting our shoes wet. We eventually found the waterfall, and yes—it was very nice. We took some pictures and then our two guides helped us get back to our starting point, where we paid them a few Nuevo Soles for their trouble.

Sometimes a venture seems daunting, and you don't know if you have what it takes to get to the goal. It helps to have someone to point out the trail and help you find your footing. Jesse's purpose in writing this book was to provide encouragement and guidance for a person who is interested in missionary service, but doesn't know where to start, or views the prospect as far beyond his or her ability. A series of simple steps are described in the early chapters, steps that could help a prospective missionary find God's path for him or her.

-Peggy Covert-

Jesse Mattix & Peggy Covert

Reviews

Stepping into Missions is a valuable resource for those who are interested in serving the Lord through overseas missions. This book is a good resource for potential missionaries of all ages, especially young people who are deciding how they want to spend their time, money, and resources in serving the Lord. It offers glimpses into the day-to-day lives of missionaries, and the joys and challenges that come along with living in a different culture. The relatable story-telling component and relevant questions at the end of each chapter allows the reader to think critically about weighing the pros and cons of being an overseas missionary. Thanks for letting me read it!

- Rachel Joe -

****

Stepping into Missions promises to be an excellent resource for young people interested in Christian service overseas, especially in a Latino context. Jesse speaks from experience through fascinating stories about the practical challenges and blessings of short-term trips as well as lifetime missionary service.

This isn't a book on missiology, but it gives a realistic review of the practical side of missions. I would recommend it to any who sense the Lord's calling to Latin America or are evaluating what it would take to serve there.

- Aaron Campbell -

****

Stepping Into Missions provides the reader with an entertaining but realistic and up-close narrative highlighting mission life and work, especially pointing out the complexities which can arise over the course of several years and during differing stages of a foreign missions experience. Particularly helpful are the reflection questions at the close of each chapter which encourage the readers to investigate for themselves the issues explored, challenging them to formulate their own more informed ideology for approaching or understanding missions.

- Hannah VaLeu

Stepping into Missions was an engaging and thought provoking read. The workbook / reflective style paired well with the narrative, complementing each other with clear purpose. The story helped contextualize its questions, and I found the pairing leading me to honestly give the questions thought. The broad timeline covering the lives of these fictional missionaries brought me to consider new aspects and problems of missionary life, ones that I might have briefly encountered before, but now began to supply what **I** might do. I can say that the book definitely accomplished its goal in me, and find it quite easy to assume that it would do so for others.

- Isaiah Magnuson

****

I love that ***Stepping into Missions*** presents relatively ordinary people living relatively ordinary lives as the main characters who eventually decide to go into missions. The book is written—because of the authors' experience—with a full and practical understanding of life as a missionary, complete with joys and sorrows, comedic moments and stressful scenarios—and all of the repetitiousness of daily life that happens in between. This helped me to see past the grand stories of famous missionaries we most often hear about—Hudson Taylor or Jim Elliot for example—and know that it doesn't necessarily take great charisma or an infectious, dynamic personality to become an overseas missionary. Whether this is comforting or terrifying is up to you; but this book helped me to think more soberly and clearly of what it means to be called, as a Christian, to a missional life—overseas or otherwise—and that overseas missionaries are people too.

- Naomi DesChane -

1

Meeting a Real Live Missionary

It was a beautiful day in California and Pete was enjoying the breeze as he drove along with his sun roof open. He would have preferred to be driving a muscle car, but the Honda would have to do for now. He appreciated the fact that his parents had loaned him the money to buy it during his senior year, and now he had paid them back. The Honda was all his and, after two more years of computer engineering classes, Pete could look forward to a well-paying job and a better car.

Right now, he was looking forward to an evening with friends from his church college & career group. Some of the guys were getting together to watch the new block-buster movie that everyone was talking about. However, before that event there was one pesky detail to take care of. His parents had urged him to be present at the quarterly missions meeting at church. It seemed kind of crazy to Pete—who schedules a meeting for 4:30 on a Saturday afternoon, anyway? But, at least it would be over early enough for him to meet his friends at the theater.

As he pulled into the church lot Pete was surprised that almost every parking place was taken. He noted that most of the cars were unfamiliar to him—"*Must belong to people from other churches,*" Pete thought. After closing the sunroof and brushing his hair back, Pete walked into the building, feeling something like a stranger in his own church.

The foyer was noisy and crowded with people happily greeting one another. They were mostly older people, and from the conversations going on around him, Pete guessed that most of them saw each other only at these inter-church missionary meetings. Pete felt awkward, with no one to talk to. Looking across the room, he saw someone else who looked alone and awkward. The guy was wearing a suit coat and tie, so Pete figured he must be the missionary speaker. Pete thought someone should talk to the guy, but not him—he had no idea what to say to a missionary. Instead, he headed for the refreshment table and got some chocolate chip cookies. As he turned away from the table, Pete bumped into Alex—the only other young person in sight. Pete and Alex had attended summer camp together when they were kids, so this was a good time to catch up with each other. Pete was surprised that Alex regularly attended these missionary meetings and had even gone on a short-term mission.

Alex was just starting to tell Pete about his mission experience when someone blinked the lights—a signal for everyone to move into the auditorium and sit down. On the stage someone was tuning a guitar and two other guys were huddled around the missionary's laptop computer, trying to figure out how to connect it to the church's AV system. One of them looked around kind of helplessly, and then spotted Pete and Alex; since they were young guys, they must know how these things work. Next thing Pete knew, he had been drafted to help out. *"Okay, Mr. Computer Engineer,"* Pete told himself, *"you just got a job, and you can forget sitting in the back row and getting a little shut-eye".*

Pete and the missionary, whose name was Mr. Conrad, had a hurried conversation while Guitar Man led the congregation in a couple of choruses. To his surprise, Pete found Mr. Conrad to be a friendly, humble guy who really seemed to appreciate Pete coming to the rescue. After Pete got the laptop synced up with the church system, Mr. Conrad asked if he would help out by advancing the slides on the Power Point presentation. Pete chose an option that allowed him to preview the next slide in the series. That helped him keep pace with Mr. Conrad, so the missionary didn't have to keep saying, "Next slide, please."

As Mr. Conrad talked, Pete found himself becoming more and more interested in what he was saying about his work in Paraguay. Pete had never really thought about what missionaries do all day, and he could not have imagined what Mr. Conrad's life was like: driving on almost impassable roads, eating all kinds of strange stuff, pulling teeth for people who had never seen a dentist in their lives. And some of the answers to prayer he told about sounded like something from the book of Acts: people healed, people delivered from evil spirits, and serious accidents averted.

By the time they got to the last slide—the stereotypical tropical sunset scene—Pete was buzzed. A million questions were bouncing around in his head and he could hardly wait to quiz Mr. Conrad. Unfortunately, it seemed like everyone else had the same idea and a crowd of twenty or more people were gathered around the speaker. Pete joined the questioners surrounding Mr. Conrad as they moved slowly toward the foyer and then out on the porch. Some of Pete's questions were answered as he listened to the discussion, but there were other things he wanted to know. He waited patiently, knowing he'd have the "last word" since he was still holding Mr. Conrad's laptop.

When the group finally dispersed, Mr. Conrad turned and thanked Pete for his help with the computer. Unfortunately, Mr. Conrad was late for a dinner appointment, so he could not continue talking with Pete. He suggested Pete pick up one of the prayer cards he had left in the church, and then they could be in touch by e-mail. When Pete returned with the prayer card, almost everyone had disappeared and his Honda looked lonely, at the far end of the parking lot.

As he pulled out onto the street Pete glanced in the rearview mirror, admiring the sunset, though it was not nearly as dramatic as Mr. Conrad's last picture. Heading home, Pete suddenly remembered that he was supposed to be going the other direction to meet up with his friends. He had totally forgotten the movie and now, with traffic getting heavy, he would be late. He quickly stopped at a strip mall and texted one of the guys to tell him that something had come up and he was going to skip the movie.

Arriving home, he found his mother unloading the dishwasher. She was surprised to see him, thinking he wouldn't be home for hours. Dinner was over, but there was some ham in the fridge and she said Pete could make himself a sandwich. He quickly slapped the sandwich together and looked for his favorite drink, a Dr. Pepper—just one left. Picking it up, he asked if he could take the food to his room where he wanted to look up some internet information about Paraguay.

"Oh, Pete—you're not thinking of going there, are you? Did you see that picture of a tarantula?" his mother asked. Pete's dad chimed in, "Son, don't do anything rash. Remember you have two more years of college. You don't want to waste all the time and money you have invested."

"Don't worry," Pete replied. "I just thought Mr. Conrad's presentation was interesting and I want to check some of his facts." Taking the stairs two at a time, Pete went to his room. As he booted up his computer, a strange thought went through his mind: *"I wonder if they have Dr. Pepper in Paraguay?"*

Observations

The idea of "being called to the mission field" has a certain mystique about it. Stories about a clear and almost mystical call are well known and make an interesting introduction to a missionary's autobiography, but is this the norm? Likely, many missionaries have had a much more prosaic experience, perhaps a slow unveiling of God's will over months or even years. Some might not even remember the stirring of heart that was the beginning of a journey of seeking after the Lord.

Many missionaries can look back to an experience such as the one in our story that started them on the path to overseas service. Often, it is a veteran missionary who catches the attention of a young person and inspires him. The missionary may have an enthusiastic personality that creates excitement, or perhaps something entirely different, a quiet sense of purpose and depth of character that attracts a young person who is seeking God's will. In any case, it is more than the missionary's personality; it is a work of God who is using the missionary as his tool at that moment.

Pete's first impression of Mr. Conrad was somewhat negative: he was only person wearing a tie, and he looked awkward standing alone across the room. As they worked together to get the computer connected, Pete warmed to the man's personality. Then, listening to the presentation, Pete was bowled over by the amazing experiences and answers to prayer that seemed to be normal for Mr. Conrad.

Regarding the missionary meeting Pete attended, there are many aspects of it that could be criticized. There seems to be a lack of organization: no one worked with the missionary ahead of time to find out what kind of technical help he might need. In fact, no one seemed to pay any attention to him before the meeting. The attendees are mostly older people; the only two young people in sight are Pete and Alex.

Questions:

1. What stories have you heard or read about how God called people into His service?

2. If Pete is truly interested in some kind of overseas experience, what are some steps he might take to move forward?

3. What are some factors or people that might dampen his enthusiasm?

4. Should the missionary meeting format be changed to attract young people? How?

5. What do older attendees at a missionary meeting have to offer, since they are generally not candidates for overseas service?

Jesse Mattix & Peggy Covert

2

That First Mission Trip

The plane was on final approach and Pete was a bit nervous. He had been on a number of flights before but had never landed at a high-altitude airport like Quito. Being an airplane buff, Pete knew that high altitude landings are tricky; the thin air means the plane has to come in at a high rate of speed. Not only that, but Quito's runway was only 10,000 feet long and he had read about planes overshooting the runway and crashing into nearby buildings. Cinching up his seatbelt a notch, he glanced out the window as the pavement came up to meet them and they went barreling down the runway, finally stopping at the far end.

As they taxied back to the terminal, Pete turned to his seat-mate, Alex, and said, "Praise the Lord—we had a safe landing!" Alex smiled and said, "You kind of had that 'white knuckle' look as we were coming in." It was Alex who recruited Pete to join this mission team. After getting reacquainted at the missionary meeting in the spring, they had gotten together a number of times. Alex's enthusiasm for missions was contagious and meshed with the interest that Mr. Conrad's presentation had kindled in Pete.

Fortunately for Pete and the other six team members, Alex was a veteran of several mission trips to South America and knew the drill; in fact, he was the official team leader. Before the plane landed he guided them through the process of filling out embarkation cards, reminding them that the flight number was AV8372, and explaining that the mysterious word "apellido" meant last name, not first name.

The plane was still on the taxi way and the "fasten seat belt" light was on, but most of the passengers were on their feet, opening overhead bins and hauling out their stuff. Pete and his group stayed seated until the plane came to a stop; as a result they were the last ones off. Walking down the stairs to the tarmac, Pete took a deep breath. The morning air was surprisingly cool and Pete had the troubling feeling of not being able to get enough oxygen—a reminder that their location was almost two miles above sea level.

In the terminal they went through immigration and picked up their checked bags. Alex guided them to the green exit which meant "nothing to declare". Out on the sidewalk they were surrounded by taxi drivers who desperately wanted their business, but fortunately, Mr. Edgren, their host missionary appeared just then and guided them to his Eurovan. Somehow, they packed in all the luggage and passengers and were soon on their way. Mr. Edgren explained that they would be staying at the mission guest house in north Quito, just a few kilometers from the airport.

Looking out of the van window, Pete was surprised to see how modern and nice this part of the city appeared. Most of the buildings in the area were one or two stories tall and usually surrounded by high walls. The street they were traveling on was wide enough for two lanes in each direction, but sometimes cars crowded in, three abreast. The grass median in the middle of the street seemed to be a place where peddlers set up shop, trying to sell various things to people driving by. When they stopped at a traffic light, a young boy began washing the van's windshield. He managed to rub his rag over the left half before the light changed. Mr. Edgren opened the window and handed the boy some change before starting through the intersection.

A few blocks later the van slowed down. A gate on the right opened and Mr. Edgren drove into a pleasant courtyard with colorful flowers all around the edges. The guest house was an older building, two stories, topped by a long, sloping tin roof. Two men in coveralls appeared and started unloading the van, hauling all the luggage inside. They were friendly, smiling and saying, "Bien venidos, hermanos!"

Mrs. Edgren, the mission hostess, welcomed the team. As she led them upstairs to their rooms, she cautioned them to take the stairs slowly. "Until you get used to the elevation, it is best to go slow—we don't want anyone fainting" she commented. She showed them to their rooms, and Pete was glad that he would be sharing a room with Alex. Mrs. Edgren suggested that, rather than unpacking, they should rest until lunch, which was about an hour away.

Lunch turned out to be more like dinner—the main meal of the day. The first course was soup, followed by the second course, some kind of meat, with potatoes, and other vegetables. While they were eating the phone rang and Mr. Edgren went out into the entry hall to answer it. The team could hear him saying, "Claro…claro."

When he returned, Mr. Edgren said, "Well, that is kind of unfortunate, but I think we can figure out some kind of 'plan B' for you folks." The team members had been planning to paint classrooms in the nearby school for missionary kids, and then lead a Vacation Bible School in the late afternoons. Mr. Edgren explained that there was a problem: for some reason, the paint they needed was unavailable. What was available was either the wrong color or the wrong quality.

"Looks like you won't be able to paint, but I know of another work project you could do. However, it is about five hours' drive from here. There is a little village out to the west, near Santo Domingo, where we started a little church. The folks there are meeting in a run-down adobe building but have been able to save up money to buy some concrete blocks. I think they would love to have some help replacing a couple of walls."

Alex looked concerned. "Sure, we could do a different project in a different place, but what about the VBS we were going to have? Won't you have a lot of disappointed kids here?"

"I'm not too worried," Mr. Edgren replied. "Folks here don't plan ahead a lot, and likely most of the kids didn't know you were going to have activities for them. Plus, another mission team is coming in about three weeks, and they could provide a VBS program—I'll ask them to do that. Besides, you can do your VBS program in San Miguel. In fact, that would be a real boost for the church down there, to have some foreigners come and do something to attract kids, get them into the church where they could hear the gospel...Why, I think this could be a real Romans 8:28 occasion!"

A couple of the team members looked blank, so Alex explained: "You know, 'All things work together for good'; that's Romans 8:28."

Mr. Edgren was in high gear now, figuring out how everything was going to work. "Let's see...you'll need work gloves. We can stop at the hardware store tomorrow and get some. This afternoon we should go to the Mitad. I'm afraid it will be your only chance to see it." Looking around the table and seeing puzzled expressions, he explained, "The Mitad del Mundo—the middle of the earth. It is probably the best tourist attraction in Quito. You know, we're right on the equator here. People love to go to the Mitad and get their picture taken with one foot in each hemisphere. Also, there is a first-class museum of Indigenous Peoples, plus lots of shops where you can buy souvenirs."

At the mention of souvenirs, Nancy and Grace, the two girls on the team, perked up; they had been looking a bit drowsy after staying awake the entire flight, watching movies. It sounded to the rest of the group that there was something of interest for each of them at the Mitad, so they quickly got ready to go.

It was almost sunset by the time they finished exploring the Mitad, and totally dark when they got back to the guest house. Pete remembered reading that there is almost no twilight in the tropics. Funny, Quito didn't really seem like it should be in the tropics; in fact, as soon as the sun went down the air became chilly. Back at the guest house Mrs. Edgren had a simple supper waiting for them. By the time they finished, everyone was ready to call it a day.

The next morning Alex gathered the team in the living room for a devotional time before breakfast. He did his best, but Pete noticed that everyone seemed kind of distracted. *Too many new experiences,* Pete guessed. Breakfast was simple—panecillos (little rolls) with butter and jam, plus coffee and some kind of fresh fruit drink. The coffee smelled good, but Pete knew from experience that he wouldn't like the taste, so he chose the fruit drink—delicious. Nancy and Grace were really into coffee, and Pete figured it would keep them wired for most of the day.

After loading up the van and saying goodbye to Mrs. Edgren, they were off. First stop—the ferreteria, aka, hardware store. "We'll stop at the one on Seis de Diciembre" Mr. Edgren told Alex. "December 6 is the name of the street. In South America many streets are named for famous dates, though I suspect many people don't know the meaning of most of them. However, this one is well known—December six is Quito Day because that was when the city was founded in 1534."

At the hardware store Pete was surprised by two things: how small the place was, and how much stuff was on display. He also noticed that many things were fastened down; one wall was covered with tools that seemed permanently attached. It appeared that customers could look for something they wanted, then ask the clerk to get one just like that...from somewhere. The team managed to get enough work gloves—in the right sizes—for all of them, and then they were off, finding their way through the chaotic morning traffic.

Heading west from Quito, the highway went steadily downward and soon everyone was shedding sweaters and jackets. Midmorning they stopped in a small town and enjoyed fruit drinks at a roadside stand. By noon they were on the outskirts of Santo Domingo, and the weather was really tropical—hot and humid. Mrs. Edgren had packed sandwiches, which they enjoyed at a quiet place next to a stream. It was late afternoon when they arrived in the small town of San Miguel. Mr. Edgren parked the van in the town plaza and everyone got out to stretch and look around. On one side of the plaza was the Catholic church—the biggest structure around. Opposite was the town's only hotel, El Carmen, which looked old and tired. Checking into the hotel, they went up a creaky flight of stairs to rooms on the second floor. The place was certainly a bargain, $10 for each of the double rooms. Of course, amenities like soap and toilet paper were lacking. Fortunately, Alex had warned everyone to bring their own.

By the time the team got settled in their rooms, it was getting dark. Mr. Edgren led them to a restaurant a block off the main street. It was a small, dimly lit place featuring wood tables with greasy plastic covers, and flies resembling air traffic at a busy airport. There was an embarrassing moment as everyone became adjusted to the dim light and noticed the décor—large, full-color ads for beer, soda, motorcycles and more, all of them featuring scantily clad women. Mr. Edgren seemed oblivious, and Alex, who wasn't surprised by the soft porn, quietly told the group to sit down and study the menu. In spite of first impressions, the food turned out to be good and plentiful.

While they were eating, a tall young man walked into the restaurant and greeted Mr. Edgren enthusiastically. "Don Roberto!" Mr. Edgren exclaimed before he introduced the newcomer to the group. He explained that don Roberto was a member of the church and also a school teacher. "Don Roberto speaks English and will be happy to translate for you at the meeting tonight." Nothing had been said earlier about a meeting, and it hadn't crossed the minds of any of the team members to be looking forward to anything but a shower and a good night's sleep. Hopefully, the meeting wouldn't last too long.

The group filed out of the restaurant and followed Mr. Edgren and don Roberto down the street to the church—a rather run-down structure barely visible in the darkness, being illuminated only by two florescent light fixtures. Inside, a dozen or so people were sitting on wooden benches, obviously waiting for something to happen. When the team walked in they were greeted with a chorus of "Bien venidos!" as everyone rushed over to shake hands, or give a hug. Someone started playing a guitar—the signal for everyone to sit down and sing. After a half hour of singing Mr. Edgren whispered to Alex that it was time for him to give a talk. Alex thought quickly and remembered the devotional he tried to share with the team that morning. Maybe it would go better with this group. He started rather hesitantly but found that don Roberto was an excellent translator and the two of them quickly developed a rhythm.

After the meeting some of the men tried to explain the construction project to the team. It helped that they had already gotten started, so the process was easy to visualize. It was getting late and, one by one, people left the church saying "Hasta mañana". Pete and the other team members were only too happy to head back to the hotel and get some rest.

Entering their room, Pete had a sinking feeling as he looked toward the window, covered by a flimsy curtain. He hadn't noticed before that the room was on the front side of the hotel, right next to the huge blinking neon sign that said "Hotel El Carmen". Sleep would probably be elusive, at best, and it didn't help that the ceiling fan was barely rotating. Just then a more serious problem cropped up; one of the fellows came into their room to report that the toilet at one end of the hall was plugged up and would not flush.

"Oh, no," Alex groaned. "I forgot to tell you the most important rule in a place like this: never, never put toilet paper in the toilet—put it in the waste basket. Well, I think we're stuck for tonight. Everyone will have to use the toilet at the other end of the hall. In the morning I'll talk to the manager and see what can be done."

In spite of the blinking light and creaky fan, Pete dropped off to sleep and the next thing he knew it was morning. Mr. Edgren appeared and told everyone that breakfast would be around the corner at a little street-side eatery. It seemed strange to sit on little stools on the edge of the road and eat…whatever it was. After a quick stop at the hotel to get their work gloves and other equipment, the team arrived at the church where two older men were working. The plan was to put in as much time as they could before the day got too hot. Soon everyone had a job to do, carrying blocks, moving sand in wheelbarrows, and mixing cement.

Mid-morning, Alex thought it was time for a break. He took the girls with him to a nearby store and they returned with two-liter bottles of soda and a bag of very flimsy plastic cups. As Pete looked over the variety of flavors, Alex read his mind and said, "Sorry, Buddy. No Dr. Pepper in this little town. You'll have to drink the local stuff—it's GMT." Pete remembered that acronym: Good Missionary Training.

Giving Alex a rye smile, Pete replied, "Yeah—I guess this could be called 'suffering for the Lord' couldn't it?"

Two ladies from the church arrived with a big pot and bags of vegetables, along with a one-burner gas stove. By one o'clock their stew smelled good and everyone was ready to take a break and enjoy lunch. After lunch it was just too hot to go back to work, so the team was relieved when Mr. Edgren told them that they would return to the hotel for showers and a rest. Later, around four in the afternoon, they would be back at the church to kick off their VBS program.

The VBS turned out to be a resounding success. It seemed that every kid in this small town was there. Alex, with don Roberto translating, taught a Bible story each day and the rest of the team helped with games, crafts and crowd control. It was amazing that even the oldest kids were happy to color Bible story pictures, and all were cooperative about sharing the crayons and other supplies which turned out to be barely enough to go around.

The team sent the kids home at dusk and thought they were through for the day—not! Don Roberto informed them that the young adults from the church were planning to meet in the plaza after supper and do some singing. Did the team have any skits they could share? Three of the team members had some experience with mime and were able to scavenge the needed props.

And so the week went on with construction work in the morning, VBS in the late afternoon, and singing and mime in the plaza in the evening. Mr. Edgren was unable to stay the whole time—he had to go back to Quito on Wednesday. He planned to return Friday night, and then take the team to Quito on Saturday in time for their midnight flight.

By Saturday morning the construction work was looking good and the ladies put together one last lunch for the team and the church members. Good-byes were said, there were lots of "abrazos" (hugs) and even a few tears. Pete and the other Gringos felt like they were leaving family behind, even if they couldn't pronounce some of their names. As the loaded van drove slowly down the main street, they felt like celebrities, with most of the town waving and shouting good-byes.

On the long drive back to Quito Alex and Pete sat in front with Mr. Edgren and did a debriefing while the rest of the gang dozed in the back seats. When they arrived in the city, it seemed like an ultra-modern metropolis, almost overwhelming with all the lights, sounds, commerce and people. Mr. Edgren took them to a classy looking mall where they celebrated with a meal at Burger King. Pete was thrilled that they had Dr. Pepper, and he went back for two refills.

When Mr. Edgren dropped them off at the airport, Pete was amazed at what a clean, modern facility it was. Thinking back to his first impression—just a week ago—he could hardly believe he was in the same place. The thought came that tomorrow he would be home, and it dawned on him that his normal life was so distant from the reality of Ecuador. Where did he really belong? Part of him wanted to stay, but a question entered him mind: *Can you handle this kind of life?*

Observations

As foreign travel has become more accessible and less expensive, mission trips have become common, even expected for church youth groups—sort of a "rite of passage". A youth leader may feel pressured by parents who want their kids to have this experience that will help them grow spiritually.

Of course, the up-front purpose of the trip is presented as an opportunity to "bless" the missionaries and the natives by helping them in some way, possibly doing a construction project or putting on a VBS program. Regarding "blessing", it is not uncommon for people from more developed countries to feel they are somehow superior to those in "third world" locations and that they have vast wisdom to dispense to those needy people. Sometimes it turns out that those "needy people" have their own agenda, something like, "we'll treat you like tourists, show you a good time, then please leave your money and let us get on with our own projects".

So, how does a well-meaning youth leader plan a mission trip that is truly helpful to the missionary, and also a spiritually challenging experience for the young people involved? Having a good relationship with the missionary host will help avoid pitfalls. Honest communication is needed; the missionary makes it clear how a visit from the youth group could be beneficial to his work and the youth leader informs the missionary of the strengths and weaknesses of the team he will be bringing. Developing such a relationship may be difficult; some missionaries are resistant to hosting a team, feeling that it would take too much time from the ministry to baby-sit a mission team.

If the youth leader forms a partnership with a missionary with a view to hosting a mission team, this will likely dictate how the project moves forward. It will be a "do-it-yourself" effort with the youth leader researching travel options, visa requirements, and health concerns such as required immunizations. If the participants are mature enough, it would be good for them to work with the youth leader, helping to collect information and acting upon it.

In a case where making their own arrangements seems daunting for the leader and the group, it is possible to sign up for an organized tour. There are a number of corporations that have specialized for decades in leading mission trips. Since the organization does all the preparations, this option is going to cost more. The tour to Ecuador might run $3000 per person, while the do-it-yourself version might amount to only $1000, for tickets, passports, and project money.

Of course, even $1000 is a lot of money for young people who likely don't have much earning capacity. One of the first concerns when planning a mission team experience is figuring out how to pay for it. A popular option is for the students to send out letters, telling their plans for a summer mission trip. Some may send letters to everyone on mom and dad's Christmas card list, hoping a number of these folks will help fund the trip. While the big tour organizations consider such fund-raising efforts to be the bread and butter of being in missions, there are other possibilities. The students could be challenged to wait on the Lord, praying both for funds and for ways to earn the needed money. They might be surprised at how God chooses to answer their prayers.

Praying for funds and seeing God answer could be one of the biggest spiritual benefits of the whole enterprise, as the youth would be experiencing real missionary life—looking to God to guide and supply. Other valuable pre-trip experiences for the team would include learning about the country they plan to visit, knowing a bit about the geography and history, and especially the history of missions in that location. Ideally, the trip would be planned months in advance and during that time the team members would be encouraged to learn more about missions by reading missionary biographies, and possibly corresponding with missionaries.

Having the backing of the sending church is an important component. Unfortunately, the young people going on a mission team might see the church members as nothing more than a source of funding. Ideally, they should be much more. The church should be praying along with the young people, asking God to prepare them for the venture. Older women, "grannies", are often tremendous prayer warriors and would love to be involved in this way. Perhaps each student could be paired with an older person who would pray for and develop a relationship with the student.

When the team returns from the mission trip the church should provide opportunities for each member of the group to share his or her experience. If the young people are uncomfortable being on stage and in the spotlight, the sharing could take the form of a panel discussion, or an interview. Planning for this "debriefing" could begin ahead of the trip, with various members of the group having assignments to take photos or videos to share when they return home. The mission trip can be an encouragement to the whole church as they see themselves as a part of a greater work of God, beyond the walls of their building. When done well, a mission trip will cause the participants to have a greater sense of being contributing members of the church, and will create a greater bond between the church and the missionary who hosted the team.

Questions

1. How worthwhile are youth mission trips in regard to: individual spiritual growth of members; the youth group as a whole; the missionary host and his work?

2. If you were organizing a youth mission trip, how would you decide where to go and what activities or projects to include?

3. How important is fund-raising, and how should it be done?

4. What would you hope might be the long-term impact of the trip on the youth who participated?

3

The Mission Trip Junkie

Normally, Pete would not be thrilled to be sitting in seat 41-B on an overnight flight between Panama City and Manaus, Brazil. What made the seat in the very last row of the 767 attractive on this occasion was the passenger in 41-A, a lovely young lady named Carrie who had recently returned from her first year at a small Bible college in the Midwest. Pete, being older than her by a couple of years, had not had much interaction with Carrie in the past, but he remembered that she and her two sisters had started coming to church with their dad a few years ago. At that time Carrie's dad was a new Christian and his wife had left the family because she did not like his changed lifestyle.

Carrie's first Sunday back from Bible college, she and Pete happened to strike up a conversation. She told him that she had taken an introductory class in missions and, as a result of that class, she was seriously considering changing her major. Also, she mentioned that she had signed up to go on the church mission trip to Brazil.

Shortly after that conversation Pete phoned his friend Alex and told him that he had reconsidered, and he wanted to be part of the mission trip. Earlier, when Alex had tried to recruit him, Pete had explained that, as much as he loved South America, he preferred the Spanish-speaking countries. Brazil, where they speak Portuguese, didn't hold much appeal. Now, Pete was reconsidering and thinking that, with his growing ability in Spanish, the cross-over between languages should not be too difficult.

So, here he was, sitting next to Carrie on the overnight flight to Brazil. A veteran of several mission trips, Pete had learned how to handle these night flights: eye-shade; ear plugs; try to sleep as much as possible in order to hit the ground running. On previous trips he had shared this advice with team members, who usually disregarded it and spent the flight playing video games or watching movies on their phones. Now Pete was disregarding his own advice; he spent the whole flight in conversation with Carrie. By the time the plane landed, and he helped her get her carry-on bag from the overhead bin, Pete felt like they were in the beginning of a relationship. He hoped Carrie felt the same way.

As they went down the jet-way Pete was glad Manaus had a modern airport and they didn't have to deplane onto the tarmac and walk to the terminal. Already, he could sense the heat even though the sun had only been up an hour or so. By the time the team got through immigration formalities and baggage claim the heat was oppressive, hitting them with a humid blast that pressed down and threatened to melt them into the sizzling sidewalk. Looking around, Pete noticed that the locals were dressed appropriately for the weather, though maybe undressed would be a better term. Girls were in skimpy sleeveless tops and tight shorts. The nine gringos on the mission team were looking more than wilted and would be glad to change to lighter attire as soon as possible.

Outside the airport they ran the usual gauntlet of taxi drivers wanting to take them somewhere, anywhere. Thankfully, right on cue their host, Dr. Philips, arrived and took charge of the group. With his Hawaiian shirt, cargo shorts and flip-flops, he looked like a combination of tourist and local. His 15-passenger van was not only roomy, it had AC! Everyone relaxed and enjoyed looking at the sights as Dr. Philips drove them to the missionary guest house. By the time they settled in and had lunch, most of the team was ready for a nap.

Late afternoon, with the weather cooling just a bit, was a good time to go out and explore the neighborhood. Pete and Carrie walked a few blocks to a large plaza where they sat on a bench and enjoyed the sights, sounds and smells. Before returning to the guest house Pete helped Carrie change some money on the street for a better rate than the banks would offer. He was pleased that he was able to converse with the money changer.

Next morning after breakfast Alex led the team in a devotional. Pete observed that Carrie was listening intently, but others in the group, including himself, seemed more interested in their plans for the day. Although they had discussed the purpose of the trip a number of times, there was always the possibility of last-minute changes. When they got to the schedule for the day everyone was glad to know that they were still on track to help with construction work—actually, demolition work—at a nearby church. The Sunday school wing of the building was ancient and had a leaky terracotta tile roof. The plan was for the team to remove all the tiles. After that, the team would go up to the Rio Negro region for a couple of days to help with a medical mission while local experts replaced the roof. Then, if time permitted, the team would paint the Sunday school classrooms before returning to the States.

Today they wanted to get an early start that would enable them to make considerable progress before the afternoon heat. Alex had insisted that everyone bring long pants, gloves, and sturdy boots to wear while working at the church. The team suited up and headed to the work site where they found the youth from the church ready to help. Pete noticed that the local kids were all wearing shorts and tank tops, along with what Alex referred to as "OSHA approved flip flops". Amazingly, no one got hurt as various people tossed the tiles down from the roof while others caught them and passed them down a row of workers, ending with the tiles in a more or less orderly heap.

By midafternoon the group had made amazing progress and everyone was ready for a break. A nap in the shade would have been nice, but the church youth produced a soccer ball and challenged the gringos to a game of futbol. Pete joined in, but soon decided he needed a break. Dr. Philips had brought a cooler with some cold soda, and Pete was so thirsty he didn't care that there was no Dr. Pepper. As he sipped his drink, some activity across the soccer field caught his eye—three young gals, dressed short and tight in all respects, were heading toward him, arms linked, and kind of dancing, like they were in a chorus line. Totally engrossed in their performance, Pete didn't realize immediately that Carrie had sat down beside him until she said, "What are you looking at, Pete?" Turning toward her, Pete felt his face flush, and it wasn't just from the sun. Her look was cold, and he tried to say something humorous, but didn't succeed.

Meanwhile, the trio had arrived and was being introduced to the team. It turned out they were part of the youth group. The introductions were awkward; all Pete could remember later was that one girl was named Diana. Soon the atmosphere loosened up and the girls lost their street swagger once they joined the crowd. Pete was hoping he could straighten out things with Carrie, but she seemed to be avoiding him the rest of the day. After supper Alex pulled Pete aside and asked if he was okay. Pete mumbled some response and said he was tired and needed to get to bed early.

The following day the team was ready to go almost before sunup. Everyone was excited to be going on a real jungle river trip which involved riding several hours in a large open boat with a very noisy motor. Pete appreciated the noise—it made conversation impossible and that was fine with him. As they progressed downstream, the motor's racket annoyed numerous flocks of birds that launched out of the surrounding trees, circling around and cawing raucously. The only other wildlife in view was turtles that were sunning themselves on floating logs. As the boat passed, the turtles would disappear into the muddy water.

Dr. Philips had brought along sandwiches which the group devoured just before arriving at the first indigenous village where he had arranged to have a clinic. As the boat pulled into the port (if you could call it that—just a muddy strip of beach with a few dugout canoes) it looked like the whole village was on hand to greet the doctor and his crew. The adults spoke their native language, but most of the school kids could speak Portuguese and a few teens had learned a bit of English. Using lots of sign language, several team members managed to get the younger kids organized for some games and then activities featuring "The Wordless Book". The local school teacher translated the Bible lesson using the colors of the wordless book.

Meanwhile, Dr. Philips enlisted Alex along with Carrie and another girl to help with the clinic. Alex's main job was crowd control—keeping people in line and trying to figure out which ones had serious health problems. Carrie took notes for the doctor while the other girl handed out pills as he prescribed them—mostly Tylenol and some kind of antibiotic. By the time all the patients were seen, the team's estimation of Dr. Philips had gone up several notches. He was a general practitioner but had gained a lot of experience in dealing with tropical diseases and had an amazing ability to diagnose, even when he could not communicate with the patient.

That evening, after everyone had a chance to cool off in the river and then enjoyed the local cuisine, Dr. Philips did a Q&A with the team, sitting around in the school room with a couple of oil lamps for illumination. Dr. Philips talked about village health care and the lack of it, describing some of the difficult cases he had seen. Often, illness was made worse by the "cures" prescribed by the local witch doctor. In recent decades many villagers had become Christians; even so, it was tempting to go to the witch doctor when no other help was available. However, there were encouraging stories of miracles that had occurred in answer to prayer. Dr. Philips explained that, in this indigenous culture, there seems to be a much closer connection between the physical and the spiritual than we feel in our Western culture.

The discussion was fascinating, but eventually several people were starting to nod off. Alex handed out mosquito nets and directed the guys to spread out in the village meeting hut while the girls laid out their sleeping bags and nets in the school room. Everyone was thankful for the mosquito nets which offered a sense of security and protection, not only from the mosquitoes, but from the bats that silently swooped around.

Between sleeping on the floor and being awakened well before dawn by the village roosters, no one on the team was looking very chipper when they assembled for breakfast. The local women served some kind of hot drink that appeared to be mashed bananas mixed with some fruit juice. It was very tasty. Quickly packing their gear, the team loaded into the canoe and headed to another village, waving good-bye to their new friends until a bend in the river took them out of sight.

Two hours later they arrived at the other village where Dr. Philips had arranged to have a clinic. The activity was much the same as the day before, but went more smoothly this time, as the team knew the drill. Again, the local schoolteacher helped with the Bible lesson. Pete realized that he remembered some of the words he had heard the day before. Eventually all the patients were seen, and lunch was served—some kind of chicken soup. Once more the team had the feeling of being celebrities as they headed back upstream with everyone on the bank waving and shouting good-bye.

The trip back to Manaus was long and uneventful. Everyone was feeling stiff and sunburned when they crawled out of the boat and returned to the guest house. With nine grungy people and only two bathrooms, there was some competition as to who was going to get the first shower. A real shower in a real bathroom—total luxury, after the village experience. By supper time everyone was clean and looking more or less civilized. Alex had planned a group activity for the evening, but seeing the zombie look on various faces, he decided to skip it and encourage the team to get a good rest. Tomorrow would be another busy day.

Friday morning Dr. Philips was out early, buying paint for the Sunday school rooms. When the team got to the church, they found the new roof in place and the classrooms ready to paint. The team divided into several small groups, each one responsible for painting a classroom. Carrie and another girl began sketching ideas for murals. By Saturday afternoon all the rooms were finished, and the team had a good feeling of accomplishment. Pete made a point of complementing Carrie on the success of the murals; she accepted his praise, but still seemed kind of distant.

That evening there was a big youth event with kids from the church and others who showed up because of the foreign visitors. Everyone wanted to see the newly painted classrooms and there were lots of comments: "bonito" "lindo" and "belissimo". The group moved on to the plaza where they planned to do some singing and a few skits. Pete stood on the edge of the crowd, observing. He noticed that some of the local guys were looking Carrie over, but he ignored them. Carrie seemed to be ignoring them, too, or maybe she was oblivious.

Just then someone touched his arm. Pete looked down and saw that it was Diana, the girl he had met a few days earlier. She smiled at him and said, "I wont to praykteece Eenglesh." Pete laughed and responded, "Eu quero practicar português falando." They quietly backed away from the crowd. Pete was glad that he wasn't involved in the skits and would not be missed. He and Diana slipped down a side street and traded vocabulary words as they walked a few blocks. When they came to an ice cream vendor, he figured out how to ask if she would like an ice cream cone. After enjoying the treat, they sauntered back to the plaza, just as the team was finishing their presentation. Pete said a hasty "até mais" and Diana responded, "Tchau tchau" as she gave him a quick hug. Pete was relieved to see that the team was busy loading into the van, and no one seemed to be looking in his direction.

Sunday morning Pete and the rest of the team really enjoyed the church service, especially the singing. Some of the tunes were familiar but had been altered in rhythm to fit the local culture. Everyone was clapping and swaying—really getting into the music. Pete was standing next to Carrie and thought she seemed less icy than a few days ago. Maybe the music was having a good influence on her.

At the Sunday evening service, the musicians really pulled out all the stops with drums, guitars and a couple of trumpets. The singing was even heartier than in the morning, and there was more gyration; people were almost dancing. Pete was trying to figure out how to clap the tricky rhythm when someone came alongside and took his hand. It was Diana. Instead of her usual costume, she was dressed very modestly in a long, conservative dress.

"Vestido bonito" Pete whispered when there was a lull in the music. He was hoping she would understand that he was trying to show approval of her more modest appearance, but he soon realized that wasn't how she took it. During the next song Pete became more uncomfortable as Diana tried to get him to sway with the music. Pete was really beginning to sweat, and not just from the humidity, when Dr. Philips came to his rescue. Apparently, from his vantage point on the stage he could see what was going on. At the end of the song, he took the microphone and announced that one of the visitors was going to speak to the congregation, bringing greetings from the church that sent the team to Brazil. Dr. Philips asked Pete to come to the stage and say a few words. Fortunately, it was a long way from the back of the church and by the time he got to the stage Pete had figured out something to say. Pete stuck close to Dr. Philips for the rest of the evening and was the first one in the van when it was time to leave.

Later that night, back at the guest house, Dr. Philips took Pete and Alex for a walk around the block, just the three of them. He shared some insights about the local culture, particularly relationships between men and women. His talk ended with, "You guys have an early flight tomorrow. Pete—you may be leaving here just in time."

Observations

Admittedly, the phrase "Mission Trip Junkie" is a prejudicial term. While it is possible for someone going on multiple mission trips to be a blessing, there is also the possibility that such trips can become a hobby, with the participant having a number of superficial experiences. Or, it might amount to having the same experience multiple times. This can lead to pride and dropping your guard, spiritually. It would be fair to ask honest questions of a mission trip junkie: Why are you going on this trip? What role are you playing on the team? What do you hope to learn or observe? How do you plan to be an asset to the team?

In this chapter we noted the problem of a romantic situation developing between a team member and a local person. This is not uncommon when the visitors have not been adequately instructed about cultural differences. North American and South American cultures are very different, especially in regard to interpersonal relationships. Latin people tend to be much more relationship oriented that North Americans and more accepting of casual romantic encounters. It is easy for the individuals on both sides to get the wrong impression of what the other person is offering or expecting.

It is important for mission team participants to have some training in this area. They should know that just being an American can make them very desirable. It is not uncommon for someone to seek an American spouse in order to get a visa. Americans are assumed to have money—how else could they travel around the world? Americans are thought to be more honest and stable in romance and marriage, so if you don't want to be cheated on, hook up with an American. In addition, there is the race factor—white is viewed as better than dark skin in much of the world. This might seem puzzling to young Americans who obsess over developing the perfect golden tan.

The whole subject of male/female relationships is an area where the "mission trip junkie" could be a real help to his teammates. His prior experience might enable him to speak knowingly about the romantic pitfalls, and help people avoid them.

Questions:

1. If a church regularly sponsors mission teams, how often should any one person participate?

2. What factors might cause the leaders to discourage people from becoming "mission trip junkies"?

3. As a leader, what steps could you take to help your team understand cultural differences they might encounter?

4. If you were leading a team and saw an inappropriate relationship developing, how would you handle it? (Note: this could be a relationship between a team member and a national, or between two team members.)

5. What guidelines could you establish to help avoid romantic pitfalls?

4

Internship Experience

Pete waved good-bye to Mr. Conrad with a brave smile, while a sinking feeling crept up into his chest. This was going to be an interesting night—or possibly two, if worse came to worst. Mr. Conrad, sitting in the back of a small pick-up truck, gradually disappeared from view behind a cloud of dust. It was a blessing that the overcrowded truck had come by just a few minutes earlier and Mr. Conrad was able to hitch a ride back to Concepcion, taking with him the punctured radiator hose, alternator and fan belts. In the city he would be able to get replacements and repairs, and hopefully, return sometime tomorrow—or the next day.

Pete's task was to stay with Mr. Conrad's disabled truck, a Brazilian made Toyota Bandeirante that had seen better days. Actually, the cargo was more valuable than the vehicle; they were hauling a generator, film projector and sound system, planning to have an evangelistic meeting at one of the haciendas in this barren wilderness. So, there was Pete, in the middle of nowhere, hoping that some cattle rustlers wouldn't come along and take an interest in his equipment.

The trouble with the truck had started a couple of hours earlier when the engine developed a terrible rattle. The rattle got worse, and then, accompanied by a screaming sound, a puff of steam shot up from under the hood. Mr. Conrad was able to pull off the road and coast to a stop. Looking under the hood, they discovered that an alternator bolt had sheared off and ripped into the radiator hose, tearing it apart. One fan belt was broken and the other was shredded down to the nylon strings. Mr. Conrad was pretty clever at making do, but this problem would need more than bailing wire and string. So now he was heading back 160 kilometers to find parts in the big city. He was hoping to get the needed parts before the shops shut down, but he probably would not be able get someone to re-weld the alternator eyelet with aluminum welding before tomorrow. Then—find a ride back to where Pete was waiting.

It was disappointing that they would not get to their rendezvous at the hacienda tonight, and there was no way to notify their host. But—people in these parts tended not to worry overmuch about schedules. It something doesn't happen today, well, maybe tomorrow. Out here in the Gran Chaco cell phone service was nonexistent, so Pete's phone was not too useful, except as a flashlight, some tunes and maybe his compass app. He reminded himself to go easy on the battery, as there was no way to charge it.

As the sun slanted down toward the horizon, Pete took stock of his supplies: some heavy bread rolls and local salami meat that they had packed along for emergencies, and plenty of water. That would be important during the hot daylight hours, and he had a blanket to ward off the chilly night. He also had his thermos full of cold water so he could enjoy some tereré. Tereré, he had learned shortly after arrival in the country, was the national drink of Paraguay. It was similar to the yerba mate that was so popular in Argentina and Bolivia. However, in those countries the beverage was hot and sweet, while in Paraguay people drank it ice cold with no sugar. When Pete was in college some of his friends were into the Argentine version. There was a café near the campus that specialized in mate and it was kind of a fad for a while. Of course, being in California, they didn't just serve it plain—they offered something like 18 varieties of fruit flavored infusions. Pete tried the basic version, made with tea leaves, boiling water and sugar and was not impressed. When he first arrived in Paraguay, he didn't expect to like tereré, but it was such a part of the culture, he knew he had to try it, and surprisingly—he actually liked it, and soon was almost as "addicted" as the locals. In the hot climate the cold drink was refreshing, but more than that, it seemed to be the key to friendship—people really connected when sitting around drinking tereré. Everyone had his own cup which he carried with him. People even had cup-holders on their motor scooters and would be seen slurping the drink while waiting for the traffic light to turn green.

Thinking about tereré made him thirsty, so Pete cautiously poured some of his precious cold water from the thermos into the tall cup with yerba mate leaves in the bottom. He stirred the leaves with the metal straw that had a strainer on the bottom and then sucked in the refreshing drink—ahh! Ruefully, he thought about how the drink was said to "loosen tongues" and get conversation going. No one to talk to here, but himself. He began thinking of what had led him to be here, stuck in the middle of nowhere.

It had begun with an unlikely friendship; a gentleman in his late 70's, Mr. Edney, had taken an interest in Pete after he came back from the mission trip to Brazil. Mr. and Mrs. Edney were retired missionaries and *missions* was in their blood. If they couldn't serve on the mission field themselves, they would try to encourage younger people to join the cause. And so, Mr. Edney began phoning Pete once in a while, asking if he'd like to come over for "pie and conversation". The first time, he offered "pie and coffee" but soon found out Pete was not a coffee drinker. Mrs. Edney's pies were superb, and Pete enjoyed talking with the couple. They had hundreds of stories of missions in "the good old days", which probably weren't all that good. When they first went to the mission field, travel conditions were incredible, and communication options were just as bad. No internet, of course. Air mail took weeks to arrive, if it came at all. Sometimes they were able to connect with a friend by ham radio. Overseas travel was by ship, often by cargo freighter, and most missionaries only came home every seven years. Of course, by the time Mr. and Mrs. Edney retired, there were lots of improvements, including jet planes.

One evening the conversation switched to Pete's future plans. A recent college graduate, Pete had taken a contract engineering job to earn a living while he figured out what he really wanted to do. That evening he told Mr. and Mrs. Edney that he definitely had an interest in missions but didn't know what the next step should be. He felt that he was maxed out on short-term mission trips, but not yet ready to commit to full time missionary work He felt a pull to Latin America but had no leading as to exactly where. And—what abilities did he have that would be useful? How would he figure out what he could/should do?

Mr. Edney came up with a logical next step—something between short-term and long-term: do an internship. Pete had heard of missionary internships, but they seemed to be arranged for students at Bible colleges. How would he ever qualify for an internship? Mr. Edney thought that, even without a formal internship, there were missionaries who would be happy to have a young man come alongside and get involved. The missionary would benefit by having extra help, and Pete would learn what missionary life entails by shadowing his mentor. Pete immediately thought of Mr. Conrad in Paraguay, whose presentation at the missionary meeting had first sparked Pete's interest. Later that night Pete searched through his desk and found Mr. Conrad's missionary prayer card which included his e-mail address. Mr. Conrad quickly replied that he would be happy to take Pete on as an intern and suggested a six month stay in Paraguay during which Pete could "shadow" him and also improve his Spanish. A flurry of e-mails followed, as Pete worked through the necessary preparations.

And now, here he was, four months into the internship with maybe 24 hours of solitude in which he could take stock of how things were going and what he had experienced. Pete felt he had learned a bit about being patient and not getting discouraged when things didn't go according to plan. Take his current situation—they should have been at the hacienda by now, enjoying a barbecue meal. Today's venture had started out as an overnight trip from Concepcion to the small village of Pozo Colorado where a believer, don Herrera, had invited them to his ranch where he had some native laborers, Guarani people, doing seasonal work. Don Herrera wanted Mr. Conrad to preach to his workers, and he invited the local church from Pozo Colorado as well. Mr. Conrad was excited to see local believers taking initiative and wanting to evangelize, so he was eager to participate. Bringing along equipment to show a movie would be a special treat for these isolated folks. Pete hoped they wouldn't be too disappointed that he and Mr. Conrad hadn't showed up.

The sun was near the horizon, so Pete decided to eat his meager supper before darkness enveloped him. As he chewed the tough bread and salami he reviewed the past months. His expectation in coming to Paraguay was to learn everything he could, but things developed differently than he had imagined. Mr. Conrad did not have a set of guidelines, chores or ministries lined up; often it seemed that the man's life was dictated by interruptions and problems. How do you "shadow" someone with endless projects which he drops when someone comes by with an urgent need? It would be simple to focus on the projects—they were things you could check off and have the satisfaction of saying, "I'm finished with that." Pete had begun to see that, for Mr. Conrad, people were always more important than projects, and Pete really admired him for that.

One of the big things Pete had learned was how much work it took just to live in Paraguay, at least for foreigners. Many local people, especially out in the country, lived very simply in small houses that were quite dirty with chickens and other animals wandering through the kitchen, and the sink draining into the yard. Pete realized that such a lifestyle wasn't practical for missionaries, especially women. He could see the benefit of Mrs. Conrad having a nice kitchen to work in, and suspected that they were all healthier because of the precautions she took, soaking vegetables in bleach solution and boiling the water they drank.

And then there was the washing machine, two of them actually, that seemed to be the bane of Mr. Conrad's existence. He had explained to Pete that when they first went to Paraguay, they bought a washing machine that broke down more often than it worked right. He finally figured out that he could avoid emergency repairs by having two machines, with the hope that one would keep working while he fixed the other one. Even though he was able to keep on top of the washing machine problem, there were all sorts of other home repairs and small improvements to keep him busy. Sometimes he would hire a national to help him, but often their different standards of cleanliness and work ethic made it frustrating. Pete was able to help with some of the home repairs and he enjoyed going to the hardware shop and trying to find whatever it was he needed.

Participating in the local church was also something Pete enjoyed. He was popular with the youth group and they taught him the local slang. With memories of his trip to Brazil, Pete was careful about the friendships he made, and was especially cautious with girls. He enjoyed playing guitar but realized that several of the guys had him beat when it came to the classic Paraguayan style music. A few times he was asked to give a message to the youth group, and he tried hard to get it worked out in proper Spanish.

Now, more than halfway through his internship, Pete was beginning to realize some things about himself. Most of the time he felt comfortable with the rhythm of life in Paraguay, but sometimes he felt like a lonely outsider. He could talk about some of this with Mr. Conrad, but he didn't want to lean too heavily on him, knowing the man was overworked as it was.

Something else that was coming into focus was the impact Mr. Conrad had among the people he worked with. Early on, it looked to Pete that Mr. Conrad was spreading himself too thin and not accomplishing much for all his efforts. But as time went on and Pete's language ability improved, he was amazed as he witnessed people coming up to greet the missionary, people he had helped years earlier, who came back again, asking for spiritual guidance. Pete respected Mr. Conrad's efforts not to be dictatorial, but yet to help people make wise decisions. And then there were the projects that Mr. Conrad quietly funded, like the Christian FM radio station that broadcast over a sat link. Pete had spent some time cleaning up the station's computers and had learned some things about recording along the way.

It was dark now. The moon had not risen, but the stars were bright. Pete sat quietly in the back of the truck, listening to the humming of insects. He began thinking of the stories Mr. Conrad had told him about the Chaco War and the legends that had grown up around that part of local history. The war had been fought in the 1930's between Paraguay and Bolivia, both countries desiring this flat desert land that might contain oil. Both countries lost a lot of men and did not gain much for their trouble. Pete knew the Paraguayans thought they won, and he figured the Bolivians probably thought they were the victors. One outcome of that time was a musical genre, something like "country and western" in the States. Actually, Pete liked the haunting melodies and the stories told in the songs much better than anything he ever heard on the radio at home.

Looking up at the stars, Pete picked out the Southern Cross, as distinctive in the southern hemisphere as the Big Dipper is in the north. As he studied the constellation, he suddenly had a funny thought: *I wonder if Carrie has noticed it?* He hadn't had much contact with her since that ill-fated trip to Brazil, but he had kept track of her whereabouts and knew she was teaching school in Cochabamba, Bolivia. When they were first getting acquainted on the flight to Brazil, Pete had been impressed at what a go-getter Carrie was. She casually mentioned that, thanks to a slew of AP classes in high school, she had entered Bible college with three semesters of credit. He knew that she had gone on to earn a double major in missions and elementary education. Their paths had rarely crossed, as she had worked several summers at a camp for children somewhere in Colorado. Thanks to FaceBook, Pete had kept track of her. When she posted something on her page he would usually click "like" or whatever, hoping she might notice that he was still around, sort of.

Now his thoughts were interrupted by a low rumbling sound in the distance, somewhere off to his left. At first, he thought it might be a truck on the road, but it was late, and no one had gone by for hours. Pete began thinking of the stories Mr. Conrad had told him as they were driving through the Chaco—stories of Bolivian soldiers, stumbling through the underbrush, desperately seeking water. Of course, the Chaco war was many years ago and those soldiers must have died of thirst. So, people claimed it was their ghosts that roamed the desert at night. The rumbling was getting louder and Pete felt a prickly sensation on the back of his neck. No way could there be ghosts out there; he needed to investigate and figure out what was making that sound.

Slipping out of the truck, Pete turned on his phone light for a moment to find the pavement. Then he turned toward the east and began walking slowly, making sure to stay on the road. The sound continued ahead of him, something like feet marching and voices mumbling. Finally, hearing the noise just a bit ahead and off to the right of the road, Pete turned on his light—and saw a funny looking piglet all alone on the road, staring back at him. It was a capybara and the tracks on either side of the pavement indicated that a herd had crossed the road moments before, and then faded into the underbrush. The piglet sniffed at him and grunted his way after the herd.

By the time he got back to the truck Pete's heart rate and breathing were back to normal. So much for phantom soldiers seeking water—it was just a herd of pigs! The night was cold; Pete rolled up in his blanket and slept.

He woke at sunrise, feeling stiff and cold, but soon the day warmed up. By midday he was trying to escape the heat, sitting under a nearby tree. He had finished the salami and stale bread and was rationing the water. The cold water in his thermos was long gone. He prayed that Mr. Conrad would return soon.

Just then he heard the sound of a motor. No one had passed him all morning, but now here came a truck. It turned out to be Mr. Conrad and the mechanic he had hired to drive him all the way out here and make the needed repairs! Not only that, but his mentor had also brought an array of snacks and a fresh thermos of ice water! Pete washed down the snacks with several cups of tereré while the mechanic installed the new parts and refilled the radiator. Soon they were good to go, happy that they would be at the hacienda well before supper.

On their arrival at don Herrera's place, Pete was introduced to the landowner and his wife, who greeted him enthusiastically and then showed him around. Nothing in the place was modern, in fact everything had the appearance of being left over from the Chaco War in 1935 but seemed comfortable in a cowboy way. The word was out that the missionary had arrived, and don Herrera marshaled up the native workers for the evening meeting under a big tree next to the house. The Guarani folks came prepared with goat hides to sit on and home spun blankets for the cold.

Pete noticed don Herrera's very authoritative manner with the Guarani natives and mentioned that later to Mr. Conrad when they were alone. Mr. Conrad explained how the old way of life was slowly changing. What Pete had observed was the end of the patriarchal hacienda system, a combination of old-world feudalism and fatherly socialism. The government had implemented a new, more democratic system, but both landlords and indigenous groups gravitated easily back to the old ways because of the security and the economic factors. No matter how this might bother Pete's egalitarianism sensitivities, he appreciated that don Herrera was using his influence to preach the gospel tonight.

Observations

Internships have become common as a means of learning on the job before making a full commitment to missionary service. For some Bible colleges an internship is a required component of the missions major. Churches can also sponsor a young person's internship as a way of gauging whether he is ready to serve on the mission field. Unfortunately, there is sometimes a disconnect, with the missionary mentor not really knowing what his role is. Older missionaries who were not mentored themselves may find it difficult to mentor a new worker. Younger missionaries may grasp the idea more easily and use terminology like having an intern shadow them. When done well, with the sending college or church laying out expectations and planning checkpoints along the way, internship is a great concept. It is a good opportunity for a young person to catch the vision, with the hope of returning as a full-time missionary who has a clear idea of what the work entails.

In planning an internship, it is important to define the relationship between the missionary and the intern, and what will be expected of each of them. Naturally, this will fall to the missionary as he is the knowledgeable member of the team, knowing the situation and how an intern could fit in. Sometimes the missionary is reluctant to impose any conditions and ends up treating the intern as a guest or tourist. That relationship is suitable for a week or two but is unsustainable for a three to nine month period. A clear discussion at the outset of the internship, or before-hand by e-mail, can help provide a good experience for both the missionary and the intern.

While the stated purpose of an internship is for the intern to learn about life and service on the mission field, the young person may learn as much about himself as about the work being done. The challenges of living in a location without all the usual conveniences can bring to light some character flaws. The discipline of regular prayer and Bible study may be hard to continue in situations where the intern is bombarded by constant noise from people living in close proximity and expecting the newcomer to be always available to chat or participate in some activity. The lack of language skill can be a very big hurdle, and the intern may feel lonely, in spite of being surrounded by friendly people. Discovering the areas in which he needs to grow may be the most valuable part of the intern's experience.

Questions

1. What kinds of lessons would you expect a person to learn through an internship?

2. How would you define a successful internship? Would it necessarily result in the intern becoming a long-term missionary?

3. What personal characteristics and abilities might be needed for a missionary to be a mentor for an intern?

4. Ideally, there should be good communication between the intern and his sponsoring church or school. What would you recommend in terms of frequency and means of communication?

5

Short Term Missionary

It was a lovely Thursday morning as Carrie stepped off the bus near the entrance to Carachipampa School. Looking up at the sign over the entrance, she was amused to remember her first day here when it was so hard to pronounce "Car-a-chi-pam-pa". That seemed like such a long time ago, *almost 15 months,* and it was hard to believe that she would be going home next week!

Originally, Carrie had been expecting to spend ten months at the school, starting in September, as the school, developed to meet the needs of missionary kids, was coordinated with the American education system. Two months after her arrival, an edict was handed down from the federal government: henceforth all schools would run on the Bolivian schedule, with classes beginning in March and ending in December. Of course, this caused great consternation among the faculty and parents, and there were many late-night meetings which sometimes got pretty emotional. In the end everyone agreed that they had to comply, and the only choice was between a very short school year (ending at Christmas), and a very long one with two months of vacation in the middle. The short option was too short to cover all the required material at each grade level, and the long option would be longer than needed to get through all the textbooks. The long option was agreed on and the teachers would deal with it by using their Christmas vacation time to research enrichment material for their students to fill in the extra time. An unfortunate result of the new schedule was that most of the teachers had to apply for a visa extension, a costly and cumbersome procedure. Carrie soon learned that the best way to deal with the situation was to hire a paralegal fixer to push her document through the system. The process was slower and more expensive than advertised, but better than trying to do it herself.

Somehow, it had all worked out, the extra long school year was winding down, and now Carrie was feeling a little teary as she thought of saying good-bye to her second graders and the few good friends she had here. In some ways the time in Bolivia had been lonely, but looking back, she knew there were people she would miss.

Carrie walked into her classroom, thinking of plans for the day. Textbooks had already been turned in for inventory, so she had prepared some activities for the kids, math worksheets and coloring pages. The class would spend part of the morning practicing for Friday's closing assembly when each grade would participate with a song and recitation. The second graders had worked hard memorizing Psalm 100, and they had chosen their favorite action chorus to sing, the one about flying over the enemy and shooting artillery. It was very popular in the local Sunday schools where they sang it in Spanish; since Carachipampa was an English-language school, the kids had learned the English words. It was funny—Carrie had never heard the song before arriving in Bolivia, but she found out that her grandparents knew it. They told her that it was popular in churches in the States during World War Two. Apparently, one of the early missionaries had brought the song to Bolivia and translated it into Spanish.

The words of the chorus, "I'm in the Lord's Army" were going through her mind when Carrie set her purse down on her desk and a package of tissue and some mints fell to the floor. Turning the purse over, Carrie felt a buzz of shock followed by intense anger as she spotted the gash sliced along one side—she had been robbed! It must have happened on the bus. Ever since she had arrived in Bolivia Carrie had tried hard to follow the rules about maintaining the "Orange Alert" mindset when out in public. *Always be alert…keep track of your surroundings…don't let anything distract you.* And now it had happened, just as she was getting ready to go home. She had been robbed. She felt like crying, but that wouldn't help. Quickly she emptied her purse and took stock—the little clutch purse containing money and two bank cards was gone, but thankfully her ID card and other documents were still in the side zipper pouch. This afternoon, in addition to working on final report cards, she would have to make some phone calls to cancel the bank cards. Thankfully, her passport was in a safe place at home; losing that would have really complicated her life! Trying to calm her mind, Carrie took a few deep breaths and prayed that she could focus on her students instead of her frustrating loss.

Hearing a commotion in the hall, Carrie opened the door for her students who burst into the room, talking excitedly in a mixture of Spanish and English. Some of them were native English speakers, the children of missionaries. Originally the school had been created to meet the needs of mission families. But, over the years, Bolivians—mainly upper class people—had requested English language education for their children. It made for a funny demographic mix: the MK's were the top students, both in grades and behavior, while the Bolivians were superior socially and materially. Unfortunately, many of the Bolivian kids, coming from wealthy homes, had a sense of entitlement and were undisciplined. If they got into trouble or got poor grades, their parents always backed them up and slyly suggested that the teacher was at fault. Thankfully, the principal handled a lot of those situations and would go to bat for the teachers.

In spite of these problems, Carrie was thankful to be in a school that upheld discipline and good behavior. Her experience as a student teacher during her last year of college had been quite a shock. She had never before heard some of the foul language the students used, even children in the primary grades. They seemed to get more of their "education" from TV than from school, and the teachers often could do little but try to keep order.

Being the last regular day of classes, some of Carrie's students were dressed up, with many of the girls wearing frilly dresses. Several of them giggled as they put little gifts on her desk, mostly chocolates wrapped with a pretty ribbon. A few boys wore dress shirts and had their hair slicked back. They tended to look a little sheepish, especially Raul, the tallest boy in the class, who crushed an apple onto Carrie's desk with a look that said, "Momma made me do it". Raul had spent two years in first grade, and was still struggling to learn to read. Carrie grabbed his hand and thanked him, then said "Raul, I'm so proud of you—you have made great progress this year." Raul looked startled, then smiled. He didn't often get compliments.

After the opening exercise—singing a gospel chorus followed by "sharing time"—the children began working on a math worksheet which required them to add two-place numbers. They enjoyed the rote activity. While they were quietly occupied, Carrie's mind drifted back to her decision to come here. She had considered applying to teach at a mission boarding school in another part of Bolivia, but the isolated rural location did not appeal to her. At that school there would have been very little opportunity to rub shoulders with local people and learn their language. Carachipampa had been a good choice. She enjoyed spending the school hours with her students, but was happy to send them home at the end of the day. As for learning Spanish, that had been more difficult that she expected. Teaching, preparing lessons, and correcting homework took much of her time, and "just living" did, too; shopping for food, cooking and doing laundry were more difficult and time-consuming than she was used to.

One reason for choosing to teach at this school was that Carrie already knew a family living in Cochabamba, José and Ruth Valez. Ruth was American and had been in Bolivia for several years as a single missionary. After her marriage to José, she had moved with him to Cochabamba to plant a church in an outlying neighborhood on the far side of the city. They had two young children and Ruth was home-schooling them for their early school years. Carrie eventually became a regular at their assembly after trying some other options during her first months in Coch. Attending the Valez' church involved a long commute—two bus rides—so sometimes Carrie spent the weekend at their home. She had gotten involved in the church's activities for children, both on Saturday and Sunday. As well, she had been invited to join the music team that led the Sunday morning singing.

The weekends with the Valez family gave Carrie a refreshing change from her weekday life, and she enjoyed the homey atmosphere. Sometimes she felt a bit nosy, observing their mixed culture marriage and lifestyle. What if she were to marry a Bolivian? Would she be able to blend in to this different culture? Ruth had told a bit about difficulties in the civil realm, keeping her resident visa current, and the almost impossible task of getting a visa for José to visit the States. Two years ago she had taken the children to California to meet their grandparents, but it was a lonely trip without José, and the kids cried a lot, missing their papa.

As she thought about the difficulties of a two-passport marriage, Carrie was thankful that nothing had developed in the romance department; most of the local guys she had met were at the Valez' church, teenagers who liked to practice their English with her. She smiled, remembering attending the youth meeting on Saturday nights, where the teens would greet her with "Good night, Miss Carrie". She tried to get them to understand that you say *good evening* on arrival, and *good night* when you leave.

Even though an intercultural marriage seemed too difficult, Carrie also wondered if she would be able to serve long term as a single missionary. She had had a taste of loneliness here in Bolivia and knew it would be a struggle to live overseas alone for the long haul. Yes, it would be wonderful to serve the Lord in a missionary situation with a husband who felt the same commitment she did. But—where to find him? When she was at Bible school, most of the fellows who were serious about full-time Christian work were focused on being youth leaders, preferably at a large church that catered to young people in every respect, especially in music. Actually, as she thought about the possibilities, she remembered two guys who were interested in foreign missions—Alex and Pete. She discounted both of them, suspecting that they were planning to be "bachelors till the rapture". On the way to Brazil, Carrie felt that she and Pete had really connected, but later in the trip he seemed to be avoiding her. She had no idea what had gone wrong.

Sounds of shuffling feet alerted Carrie that most of the class had finished their math paper and were ready for something else. She passed out coloring pages, and a special treat—a small new box of crayons for each child. They were delighted to get new crayons, especially since they could take them home to use during vacation. As they eagerly began coloring, Carrie sat at her desk and drifted back to thoughts about her life in Bolivia.

Shortly after arrival, she had been given a tip about a nice but inexpensive apartment for rent in a suburb about ten miles out of the city, but only a short bus ride from the school. The name of the village was Quillacollo—another impossible name. She had written down the phonetic spelling: Kee-ya-koyo. The apartment was in a nice location and fairly spacious, though it took a while to make the place feel like home. Decorating was not a problem but getting the electric hot water shower to work, fixing plumbing problems and dealing with security issues took a long time. She had to pester her landlord on a daily basis and mostly she heard "mañana" as a response. There were still things that needed fixing after all this time, but she had learned to live with them.

The first two months in the apartment Carrie had struggled to keep up with everything—shopping, cooking, cleaning, and laundry in addition to her school work. Several faculty members recommended that she hire a maid, and suggested a good one—Maria Luisa Quispe who lived in Quillacollo. Carrie had a hard time accepting the idea of having someone work for her, but the laundry was piling up and she was getting desperate, with no washing machine. Eventually she swallowed her pride and her American sense of egalitarianism and hired Marilu. At their first meeting the young lady explained that only her *abuela* called her Maria Luisa; to everyone else she was simply Marilu. Carrie soon realized that hiring help two days a week was definitely a good decision. Marilu kept the apartment tidy, did the laundry, shopped for groceries and even prepared some meals. On the days Marilu worked for her, Carrie could look forward to a delicious home-cooked meal. Often, she asked Marilu to stay and eat with her, and they became good friends.

Carrie visited Marilu's church in Quillacollo a few times, but the people there spoke a mix of Spanish and Quechua, which was hard for Carrie to understand. During her first months in Coch she mainly attended the International Church which was conducted in English. Many of the teachers belonged to that church, so she fit right in. It was fun to sing in English and enjoy the fellowship. The preaching was based on the Bible, though it often seemed kind of shallow, and doctrine was soft-pedaled. The pastor had to be non-confrontational about doctrine if he was to survive, with the congregation from so many different backgrounds, and unity being the big rally cry. As time went on, Carrie continued to attend some special activities, mainly for the social interaction, but realized she did not want to stay in a little bubble of expats who were trying to keep Americanism alive. In the long run, the Valez' little assembly ended up being the best choice— it was a place where she could improve her Spanish and also be a help to the group.

Midmorning, the primary classes went out for recess. When her class returned, it was time to have a last practice for Friday's all-school assembly. The kids sang heartily the song about being in the Lord's Army, with exaggerated motions. Getting everyone in sync for reciting Psalm 100 was more difficult, but after two false starts they got their rhythm and said the whole thing without a hitch! Carrie was so proud of them, and was sure their parents would be impressed. When the bell rang at noon, the kids picked up their papers to take home and lined up at the classroom door. One by one, Carrie said "good-bye" to them. It would have been easy to get choked up, but she reminded herself that she would see all of them tomorrow. In the meantime, she needed to get home and finish writing comments on their report cards. But, before that she would have to make some phone calls about the stolen credit cards.

Observations

There are many opportunities in short-term missions, both for young people who want to experience missionary life, as well as retired people who are in good health and have a lot to offer. Some of the possibilities include schools, Bible schools, orphanages, hospitals, bookstores, radio stations, bush piloting, construction projects and more. Many jobs can be done without learning another language, with the short-term worker doing physical projects and thus freeing up the career missionary to be more involved with people. Most of the openings available are for volunteers who raise their own support.

In any short-term mission situation, there is the possibility of loneliness, particularly if the volunteer worker has limited ability to communicate with the local people. It is tempting to stay in a familiar English-speaking bubble, but the volunteer will have a much better experience if he or she attempts to get to know the nationals.

There are lots of legal requirements to be aware of. As the short-termer will be staying in the location longer than a summer mission team would do, a resident visa will be needed. In some situations, a short-term worker can get by with a tourist visa, but that often requires leaving the country every three months. Depending on the location and travel options, that can be expensive and time consuming.

A person who serves in a capacity that involves driving would need to get a local license, and people working in a medical field might need credentials that are recognized by the government. Dealing with funds can be complicated and the short-termer will need to work out a channel for accessing money. In many countries you take a hit when you use an ATM, or you open a bank account and take a hit with the swift transfers. Long-term missionaries have usually worked out ways to transfer funds and they will be a good source of information.

One of the advantages of a short-term project is the opportunity to experience life in another country at a deeper level than the typical two-week summer mission trip which offers little opportunity to get out on one's own and make mistakes. The person who stays long enough to live among the people, buy and prepare food, travel on busses, and deal with another country's customs and culture, will have a much richer and perhaps life changing experience.

Questions

1. What are the main differences between an internship and a short-term mission experience?

2. If you were seeking a short-term mission experience, where would you find information about available opportunities?

3. What do you need to know before you go? List some areas of information that would help you prepare.

4. How could you prepare for emotional or social difficulties that you might experience living in a different culture?

6

Preparing for the Mission Field

Carrie was pleasantly surprised to get a phone call from Alex, inviting her to join him and Pete at *In & Out Burgers* for a mission trip debriefing. She was thankful to be feeling good enough to agree to meet the guys, since the second round of antibiotic had finally finished off whatever bug she brought home from Bolivia.

The trip home had been grueling, starting with a flight delay in La Paz that left her plane sitting on the tarmac for five hours. With the airport at 13,000 feet, she and other passengers began hoping that someone would deploy the oxygen masks. Eventually they were on their way, but of course, she missed her next connection in Houston. In the States, holiday travel crowds, plus a major storm that shut down O'Hare and messed up flights over half the country, made for a totally miserable trip. By the time she landed at LAX, Carrie was seriously ill. She had gotten run-down in Bolivia, and the long trip home was the last straw. Her sisters picked her up at the airport and made a stop at an Urgent Care clinic on the way home. A couple of prescriptions eased the misery, but even so the whole holiday season went by in a blur. Now, in mid-January, she was finally feeling well enough to enjoy some social activity.

Alex came by at noon on Saturday and took Carrie to the burger place where Pete met them. They hadn't been together since the Brazil trip, so conversation was a bit strained at first, but by the time they got their burgers and found a place to sit, the atmosphere had warmed up. In fact, they found so much to talk about that they finally decided to move on to a coffee shop down the street, having overstayed their welcome at the busy burger place.

Pete and Carrie tried out their Spanish on each other, and Carrie decided that Pete was miles ahead of her, even if he had a funny accent. They traded a few anecdotes; Carrie told about getting robbed on the bus, and Pete shared his adventure of spending the night alone in a broken down truck with only a herd of wild pigs for company.

Meanwhile, what had Alex been doing, Carrie wanted to know. She hadn't heard that he was now into mission trips full time, working for a big company called "Teen Treks". He pulled out a brochure that he had designed, which described over a dozen options for summer team mission trips. Across the top of the brochure was the Teen Treks slogan, "Boot Up 2 Serve!" Alex mentioned that all the kids who go on a Teen Treks mission trip are required to wear heavy work boots because they mainly do construction projects, such as building simple concrete block houses in third world countries.

Alex went on to explain that Teen Treks was a full-time job for him. In the fall he had visited six different countries, scoping out possible options for next summer's mission trips. In the spring he would be doing promotional work, meeting with youth pastors who might be interested in planning an overseas trip for their kids. And, of course, in the summer he would pursue what was really his first love and where he felt his gifting was, leading groups on these trips. Since he was based in the States he was considered "office staff" and didn't have to spend a lot of time raising support, like some of the missionaries he had met in the last few months.

Pete was back by this time, having gone to the counter to pick up their order—lattes for Carrie and Alex and an ice-cold caramel frappé for himself. He jumped into the discussion, commenting that "raising support" was not the only way to go. Both Mr. Conrad and Mr. Edney had amazing stories of trusting God to supply their needs and learning over and over that God is faithful.

"Besides," Pete added, "these guys have experienced God's guidance by what He supplies and what He doesn't. Mr. Conrad at one time really wanted an airplane, to speed up traveling in the Chaco, but the funds didn't come in, so he realized it was not God's will, or at least it wasn't His timing."

"So, how do people like Mr. Conrad get funds?" Carrie asked.

"It's pretty amazing," Pete replied. "You probably know that our church regularly sends funds to a number of missionaries in different countries. The money is sent to a service organization that maintains bank accounts for people who are sent out by churches like ours. Every month each missionary gets a statement telling how much money is in his account, and where it came from—which churches or individuals sent something to him. The amount of money can vary widely from month to month—that is where 'living by faith' comes in."

"Hmmm…" Carrie mused, "That sounds like a good way to go. I met a teacher at Carachipampa who belonged to a mission that requires a certain level of monthly income before a person can go to the mission field. She spent two years trying to get the needed support before she could start teaching. The funny thing was, I was able to live on about half the amount she was required to have."

"That's bureaucracy for you," Alex chimed in. "A one-size-fits-all policy set up by someone who may not know the particular situation. I see what you're saying, Pete—trusting God to meet your needs rather than an organization telling you what you need. Sounds like a good way to go."

"So—why don't you?" Carrie asked.

Alex took a long sip of his latte before answering. He explained that Teen Treks was more like a business than a mission board. The organization charged for their services and paid him a salary. "It's not a lot of money," he commented, "but, I can survive by doing free-lance graphic design in my spare time." He went on to say that he could imagine a future where Teen Treks would want him to focus on one country and spend most of his time there, setting up projects and hosting groups from the States. "In that scenario, I might be considered a foreign missionary and might need to raise support. I guess I'll cross that bridge when I come to it."

Pete wondered who Alex would call on for support if/when he crossed that bridge, and Alex assured him that, with all the mission trips he had led, there were quite a few people he had clicked with. He was sure most of them would be happy to join his support team. Pete tried to point out that support was not just money; it would be good to have people who could offer advice and who would hold you accountable. He concluded, "Money aside, I think it is critical to have the backing of your local church, with people who really know you, people you can call on for advice."

Everyone was silent for a few moments, and then the conversation took off in a different direction: Besides having some means of financial support, what else is needed to become a missionary?

Some of the ideas that popped up included:

- --Seek God's guidance as to where you might serve

- --Get your church behind you

- --Investigate visa requirements

- --Get language training

- --Pay off debts

- --Consider whether to be a "lone eagle" or join an established work

- --Get married

The last item, suggested by Pete, was a real conversation stopper. While the idea hung in the air, Pete slurped the last bit of his frappé and rattled the ice in the bottom of the cup. Carrie stared out the window, watching the traffic going by, and seemed a million miles away.

Finally, Alex came to the rescue and asked, "So, Carrie—does this mean you will marry me?"

At that, Carrie snapped out of her reverie and punched Alex on the arm, "No way!"

All of them laughed. Since the subject was now on the table, Carrie opened up about the struggles she had with loneliness in Bolivia. She had purposefully stayed away from any romantic entanglements, knowing that the path Ruth and José followed was not the way she wanted to go. Alex and Pete were philosophical about the subject, thinking that marriage was kind of optional; it might be helpful, but they could see some advantages in being single.

Pete introduced a new topic: what kinds of skills might be helpful, and what kind of training would be required? Being a trained teacher had opened the door into the mission field for Carrie; Pete's computer training could be helpful but wasn't such an obvious fit. In his mission teamwork, Alex had picked up a number of practical skills in construction and other areas. He commented that such skills are really just a means to the end which was: reaching people with God's Word. So any skill you can pack along that will help you reach people is a good thing to have.

They were on a roll now, thinking of useful skills. Someone suggested knowing how to pull teeth—seems like all the old-time missionaries did that, for some reason. The guys thought that basic mechanical knowledge was high on the list of skills, while Carrie suggested that knowing how to cook from scratch would be helpful. Basic health care and nutrition were also on her list. Alex mentioned communication and computer skills, and then came up with something unexpected: all-terrain survival skills.

Pete brought up the idea of Bible training and wondered how much is enough? Alex saw a minimal need, just preach the Gospel, give them a Bible and then steer them to a good church. Carrie disagreed; she pointed out that this was a short-term mission team mindset, not really suitable for a full-time missionary. Pete sided with her, saying that the great commission involved a lot more than handing out Bibles. Baptizing implied starting churches, and to him that suggested a need for advanced training, perhaps a master's degree, or seminary. At that point, Carrie couldn't resist pointing out that she was ahead of both of them, having a four-year Bible college degree.

Pete was about to suggest ordering more drinks—to pay the rent on the table they were occupying—but just then Alex looked at his watch. He needed to leave right now to get to a meeting with a youth group leader and wondered if Pete could take Carrie home.

Pete was happy for the opportunity, and as they walked to his car he was silently congratulating himself for having had the foresight to clean the clutter out of the Honda that morning. When he opened the passenger door for Carrie, she smiled and murmured, "Tu eres muy amable."

As he eased onto the freeway, Pete had an idea. "How would you like to go to the monthly missionary meeting, and then have dinner with Mr. and Mrs. Edney? I think they would like to get to know you."

Carrie responded, "Oh—that would be great. The Edneys seem like such genuine people—I'd love to spend some time with them."

Pete was silent as he worked his way over to the express lane, and then offered another idea. "The missionary meeting is a couple of weeks from now. In the meantime, like maybe next Saturday, we could go to this café that features Argentine style yerba mate. I think you would like it."

Carrie agreed that she would enjoy trying the traditional mate. She smiled to herself, thinking, *"I wonder how he came up with this idea...he never drinks anything hot."*

Observations

The discussion in this chapter covered a lot of general suggestions for mission field preparation, but in the end, it is necessary to zero in on what is needed, recommended, or required for the particular field where you will serve.

The would-be missionary needs to research the requirements of the organization he will work with. This might be a mission board that has very stringent rules and regulations; they might not be willing to consider anyone who does not have a four-year college degree. An advantage of joining an established mission board is the wisdom they have accrued and the oversight they provide, plus the security benefits they offer. Some missions provide an insurance package and possibly a retirement plan.

On the other hand, going out independently allows someone who believes he has been called by the Lord to go to the field with limited academic training. For such a person, starting out by working with an established missionary can help avoid a lot of trouble. Of course, it is important to develop a solid relationship with the senior missionary, either by corresponding or by visiting the field before making a long-term commitment.

An option that has been well proven by many missionaries is that of going out independently, but under the leadership of your local church and commended by them. This allows the missionary to have flexibility in terms of what kind of work he does, the timing of home visits, and what he does while in the home country. A mission board that requires the worker to raise a certain level of support will expect him to spend his furlough time doing deputation to maintain that support. The independent missionary will have the option of visiting his supporters, but with the guidance of his local church which should encourage him to get the rest he needs, and perhaps additional training.

What if you feel called to the mission field, but others—leaders in your church or missionaries you know—don't agree? This is time to take a careful look around and consider whether you are missing something important. Are you sure this is the Lord's direction in your life? Is it a time for persistence and pushing through, or should you back off? Perhaps it would be good to have a mentor who could help you figure out what is missing, or help you find a different path.

Yet, persistence, even stubbornness, is a good trait that has helped many missionaries get to the field and stay there. Being a self-starter, a person who has goals and objectives, is vital. While having such a mindset is important, the missionary also has to guard against being so project oriented that he runs roughshod over the people he came to serve. Balance is needed, to be both persistent and teachable, determined and humble.

How long to stay on the mission field is an interesting question. Traditionally, missionary service was considered a life-long commitment. However, in our current world where it is not uncommon for someone to have several careers over his lifetime, people may see five or ten years as "long term". The duration of a person's service overseas will depend somewhat on his task. A translator may feel that his job is done when he finishes a translation of the New Testament after twenty years. Someone who develops a school may pour his life into the job and "die in the saddle". Or, a missionary might plan on spending his whole life in a particular work, and then find his plans suddenly upended by illness, or by getting kicked out of a hostile country. It is important for the missionary not to focus on "doing my project" but on serving the Lord of the Harvest in whatever way He directs.

Questions

1. In the story, Pete and his friends listed ideas for missionary preparation. Which of their ideas do you think are important? What would you add to their list?

2. Many serious young Christians consider missionary service, but a large percentage of them do not actually make it to the mission field. What are some things that can hinder someone from going out as a missionary?

3. If you felt a call to missions, and people around you did not agree, you could: 1) forget about being a missionary; 2) go out on your own; 3) wait for others to agree with your sense of a call. If you chose #3, how could you prepare during the waiting period?

7

Crossing the Cultural Divide

"What about *this*?" Carrie hollered across the apartment, holding up a heavy, hand woven blanket.

"Yes, we need to take that," Pete answered, his tone just slightly less aggravated than Carrie's. Packing was such a stressful chore and made them both irritable, as they knew from past experience. It was only a year ago that they had packed up their worldly goods in California and moved to Arequipa, Peru, to attend language school. That had been a really stressful move, being limited to what they could pack in 50-pound bags to take on the plane. On their tickets, each of them was allowed two checked bags, plus one extra bag for a fee of $100. That made a total of six bags, which meant leaving a lot behind. Fortunately, some visitors came a few months later and brought more of their belongings.

Looking around the apartment at the piles of equipment waiting to be packed, Pete wondered for the hundredth time how they had managed to accumulate so much stuff. It made him think of the clutter in his parents' basement; living in the same house for twenty-five years meant his folks had collected a lot of odds and ends. *Nice thing about living in an apartment...no basement;* he mused, as his cell phone rang.

"Hola... Si, soy yo...Si, claro...claro...por supuesto..." Listening to Pete's end of the conversation, Carrie couldn't tell what was going on, but she suspected it was one of the trucking companies returning Pete's call about hauling their belongings to Chiclayo. That was another point of contention between them. Pete liked the truck idea because it was cheap and the truck could carry large items like their kitchen table and their mattress. The downside was not knowing how long it would be until their shipment was delivered. Carrie favored sending stuff by bus, which was more expensive, but more certain of arriving in a reasonable time. The bus company would not accept large items, and that was fine with her. Carrie and Pete were both thrifty, but in different ways. Pete' motto was "Keep and

Conserve". Carrie had pointed out to him that the cost of transporting everything they had acquired would make a lot of their old junk *expensive* old junk.

The kitchen table was a toss-up, regarding the value of shipping it, but Carrie really did not want to take their mattress. When they moved into this furnished apartment, they found the mattress on the bed was old and lumpy so they bought a replacement, the cheapest they could find. It was barely adequate, and Carrie looked forward to getting a better one in Chiclayo. She thought they should leave the mattress for the next people who would rent the apartment. The lumpy mattress was just one of the things they had replaced in the poorly furnished apartment, and now they had to decide what to do with everything.

Another consideration was the damage deposit that had been required when they moved in. They definitely should get it back, as the apartment was in better shape than when they arrived, since Pete had repaired all sorts of things that the landlord had ignored. In the process, Pete had acquired a set of tools; it seemed like each repair called for a different tool, and now he had quite a collection. They needed to be packed and shipped, of course. Teachers at the language school advised them to not pay the last month's rent and let the landlord keep the deposit rather than trying to haggle it out of him. Carrie felt a little squeamish about doing it that way, but maybe leaving the mattress and a few other items would smooth things out.

Pete got off the phone and reported the estimate he had received from the trucking company; he thought it was too good to pass up. Before Carrie had a chance to reply, they heard someone knocking on their door. A couple of young ladies from church had come to say good-bye. Carrie hid her frustration and invited them into the messy apartment. The girls explained that they would just stay a few minutes, but Carrie asked Pete to put the kettle on, knowing an invitation for tea would be expected. The girls offered to help with the packing, and began picking up various items, admiring them and asking Carrie if they were really going to take all these things to Chiclayo. By the time Pete came in from the kitchen with a tray full of cups and some cookies, the situation was getting on Carrie's nerves. The girls giggled their thanks to Pete, amazed to have a man serving them tea. Carrie's annoyance turned to amusement when one of the girls followed Pete into the kitchen and told him how much she admired their table. She was certain they would not want to take anything that large to Chiclayo, and if they were giving it away, she would love to have it to remember them by.

Before answering her, Pete exchanged a glance with Carrie who smiled, somewhat triumphantly. With a look of resignation, he told the girl that she could have the table if she could get someone to carry it away for her. Of course, her friend had to have some kind of "recuerdo", too, and it took a while for her to choose something that Carrie would agree to part with. Finally, they left. Pete put the cups on the tray and returned to the kitchen. Looking around at the chaos in the tiny room, he suddenly had an idea that would help both of them slip into a better mood. "Hey, Beautiful," he called to Carrie, "How would you like to go out for dinner?"

Settled into a quiet corner in the back of the restaurant, Pete quickly ordered their favorite—Lomo Saltado—and Inca Cola, the national drink of Peru. Of course, it wasn't as good as Dr. Pepper, but it was not bad if you like cream soda and don't mind the garish yellow color. Clever marketing had made it as popular in Peru as Coke was in the States. While waiting for the food to arrive they began reminiscing about their life in Peru—what they had accomplished, and what the future might bring.

Pete and Carrie were both thankful that they had spent this year in Arequipa attending Ceica Peru Spanish School. They remembered their first day at the language school, which also happened to be their first anniversary, and they had celebrated in this same restaurant. Ceica had been a good choice, both in terms of price and quality. The school had a program that took students all the way through from beginner to advanced Spanish at the student's own pace. Pete entered a few levels higher than Carrie who began at the second level, getting a good review of elementary grammar before going on to more challenging things like the subjunctive tense. Many of the teachers had evangelical church backgrounds and became good friends, taking their students on outings to markets and cultural events.

Pete and Carrie appreciated the flexibility of their studies. Since the school served the tourist market, the instructors did not mind if long-term students dropped out occasionally for a week to travel to other parts of the country. This gave them opportunities to check out ministry possibilities as they considered where they might serve in the future.

They visited Pucallpa in the jungle region of Peru, where a lot of ministries had been going on for a long time, and many missionaries were involved in village work, church planting, schools, air transportation, and more. A ministry to children in Pucallpa appealed to Carrie, but in the end she and Pete realized that the area was being well served and they should look for a needier situation.

During their time in Arequipa, they found many opportunities, both in the city and in the mountain villages of the surrounding countryside. An older missionary couple who were church planters invited Pete and Carrie to go with them to several church anniversaries in rural villages. They learned that anniversaries were a big deal, and usually called for a conference that lasted all weekend and brought in people from churches in other villages. Sometimes Pete was asked to preach at these events. It was a good workout for his increasing ability to communicate in Spanish. Carrie was able to hone her ability to communicate when the Christian grade school in Arequipa asked her to help them. Of course, they asked her to teach English, but there were still plenty of opportunities to practice her Spanish.

Two back-to-back long weekends gave Pete and Carrie time for a fairly extensive tour of the coastal region. They flew to Lima and then traveled by bus to Trujillo, Chiclayo and on to Tumbes near the Ecuador border. At each place they had some contact to visit and ministries to explore. In Chiclayo a new ministry was opening up and this caught their attention as a great starting place for them.

There they met don Guillermo, aka, Mr. Bill, who was working with some rough street kids in the beach area, teaching them skills and basic responsibility. Mr. Bill had acquired some property which included a store-front café with an apartment upstairs. Behind the building was a yard with some dorm rooms and a bakery in back. Mr. Bill was excited about the possibilities of expanding the ministry to reach out to displaced Venezuelan refugees who were flocking to northern Peru. He wanted to open up the place to Venezuelan families, giving them free rent for a month while they looked for work. The rent would increase each month until after six or seven months they would be able to venture out on their own. As one family moved out, another destitute family would move in. The guests would be given breakfast each morning, followed by a devotional time to share the gospel with them.

Mr. Bill had been praying for a young couple to come along and share his vision. He was excited by the possibility of Pete and Carrie working with him. They could live in the upstairs apartment and oversee the day-to-day activities. Carrie might be able to provide schooling for some of the refugee kids who badly needed it.

While they finished their meal, Pete and Carrie discussed various aspects of the project. As the conversation went on, Pete ordered more Inca Cola.

Another interesting aspect of living on the north coast would be the possibility of visiting the ruins of various ancient civilizations. At the language school they had taken a course in Peruvian culture and history. The teacher was excited about the subject and frequently showed pictures of interesting historical places. On their bus trip they remembered passing the ruins of Chan Chan, just north of Trujillo. It would be fun to take a closer look at that site, as well as a number of other places they had noted on their "bucket list". Of course, the biggie was Machu Pichu, with the Nasca Lines running a close second. Those two would have to wait quite a while, as they were expensive, and finances were tight—typical for new missionaries just starting out.

Thinking of the state of their finances, Carrie started having second thoughts about what they should take to Chiclayo. Maybe shipping their old junk would be better than buying new stuff. Either way, it looked like they would be living with packing box furniture for a while. Trying to make the place look homey would be a challenge. It would be tempting to use their Visa card to get things they needed, but she and Pete both wanted to follow the example of older missionaries who were guided in their spending by what the Lord provided each month.

Observations

Financial support for new missionaries is usually a hurdle, whether they "go out by faith" or with a mission board. In the latter case, they will be required to have sufficient pledges or "faith promises" to cover monthly expenses before they get the green light to go to the field. Raising support can be a slow process, testing the faith and patience of the would-be missionary. Interestingly, this type of support is often referred to as being "by faith" but it is the givers who are supposed to exercise faith, that they will be able to fulfill their pledges.

"Going out by faith" appears easier (but the fun begins when the missionary gets to the field and doesn't know from one month to the next what will be the state of his finances). Needing only a commendation from his home church, the young missionary is soon ready to board a plane and head overseas. The "letter of commendation" he has received indicates that the church is in agreement with his desire to serve on the mission field. This commendation may imply financial support, but not necessarily, or at least not enough to cover all the worker's needs. The idea is that other churches and individuals who are acquainted with the missionary will also help support him. The early years can be quite lean, but the missionary learns to trust God, and is sometimes surprised by the unexpected ways God provides.

For most people, packing is a pain, and more so for people who are planning to spend years in another country. The new worker should try to get as much information as he can from veteran missionaries or other sources that can tell him what is available where he will settle and what he might need to bring with him. Most cities nowadays have stores similar to those in the States, including huge grocery stores with names like Supermaxi or Hypermaxi. The missionary who wants to fit in and relate to the local people would do well to shop where they shop. It is nice to be able to talk with a national and share a purchase story, rather than having to admit, "I got someone to bring that from the States; you won't find it here."

Culture shock is a fact of life when a person moves to another country. Pete and Carrie had been in Peru for a year and probably thought they had gotten used to the local way of thinking. However, having guests come into their home and ask for some of their possessions left Carrie feeling upset, almost as if she had been robbed. Their time in language school and their trips around the country were a good beginning, but there was still more to learn.

Having to learn a new language can help the new worker adapt, giving him time to become accustomed to the way of life before diving into ministry. Years ago, a new worker in Uganda ended up in the hospital, suffering from stress. With English being one of the national languages, he had jumped right into a heavy schedule of teaching and preaching. Soon culture shock caught up with him and he was forced to slow down.

While it is normal for a new missionary to experience culture shock, his commitment to the Lord and to the people he came to serve should soften the impact. People who don't have that mindset may have a more difficult time. An interesting experience for me was meeting a Texan in Bolivia who had married a Bolivian woman. He actually had a siege mentality, where everyone around him was an enemy in his mind. He and his wife shared a house with her family, and he had blockaded the doors to make a separate space for himself. He made an interesting comment that explained why I did not do the same. "At least you have a reason for wanting to live with these people; I just want to be left alone."

A person who has been on the mission field for a number of years may feel that he has conquered the cultural divide, but then, shortly before furlough, culture shock kicks in as he anticipates being "home" where things just work right.

Questions

1. Imagine you were going to a foreign country to live and could take only two or three 50 pound bags. What would you consider essential to take with you?

2. Packing is stressful for most people. What ideas would you suggest for a missionary couple, or family, to get the job done without a major meltdown?

3. How important is formal language study? What are some other ways of learning a new language?

4. Have you ever dealt with a serious—or even a merely annoying—cultural difference? How did you handle it?

Jesse Mattix & Peggy Covert

8

Getting Along with Other Missionaries

During the late-afternoon lull, Carrie was cleaning up the café before the two former street boys came in to take over for the evening shift. Glancing out the window, she noticed a young woman walking slowly along the edge of the road, struggling with a baby stroller on the uneven ground. The stroller was piled high with all sorts of stuff, and Carrie assumed there was a baby in there somewhere. A small boy followed along, clutching a ragged stuffed toy. It was easy to see that they were Venezuelan refugees. But what were they doing here, on the edge of town? Most of the refugees stayed closer to the city center where there were work opportunities, rather than at this beach village.

Carrie saw the woman look up at the sign above the café that said, "Casa de Refugio" and then turn and push the stroller toward the door. By the time the woman walked into the café and asked for Señor Pedro, Carrie had figured out what was going on, and she didn't like it. It looked like another case of kind-hearted Mr. Bill happily inviting someone to stay at the Refuge, even though he knew there were no rooms available.

Calling Pete in from the yard, Carrie shared her suspicions and reminded Pete that they absolutely could not take in any more people. All the dorm rooms were full, and none of the families had gotten far enough ahead to move out any time soon. Also, Carrie had a feeling that this woman did not fit the profile of people they could help. The plan, which Mr. Bill had developed, and they had agreed to, was that they would take in people who needed help getting established and who hoped to get jobs and stay in the area long-term. They were not set up to care for transients who needed a place to sleep while on their way to somewhere else.

Pete sat down with the woman, Francisca, in the café and asked Carrie to bring her some coffee. He quickly found out that Carrie's suspicion was correct—Francisca and her children just needed a place to stay for a few days. Her story was typical; she had left Venezuela, traveling by bus, and now she was out of money. She had been begging on the street when don Guillermo told her about Casa de Refugio. It seemed like her only hope. Pete tried gently to tell her that her situation was not one that they were set up to help. Francisca asked Pete to please phone don Guillermo and clarify the situation.

Mr. Bill's phone rang way too many times before he finally answered. When Pete explained the reason for his call, Mr. Bill replied that he really didn't have time to talk. He had been invited to speak to a large church youth group and the event was already getting started. Pete wasn't surprised. Mr. Bill was an incredibly gifted speaker and churches all over town were constantly asking him to give motivational talks to their youth groups. Mr. Bill told Pete he was sorry about the mix-up; he just felt so sorry for Francisca and her little children that he impulsively told her about the Refuge, hoping Pete and Carrie could shift things around and make room for this little family. Pete replied that taking in more people was not fair to those who were already paying rent, even if it was subsidized, but he would see if they could work out something. "Fine," Mr. Bill replied. "I have to go now. I'll try to call you tomorrow."

Pete sighed and asked Carrie if she would explain the rules to Francisca while he talked to the residents and tried to find a place for her family to sleep. Francisca listened to Carrie's explanation of the house rules and expectations but insisted that she would not be staying long; she didn't seem to understand that this was the problem—the Refuge was not set up to deal with short-term people.

Soon Pete came back with the news that one of the women, Isabella, whose husband was working out of town, would be able to share her room with Francisca. It never failed to amaze Pete and Carrie that people who were terribly poor themselves were often so willing to share the little they had with others.

That evening it took hours for Pete and Carrie to calm down enough to even think about sleeping. They both felt conflicting emotions; they were humbled by Isabella's generosity and kindness, and at the same time were feeling frustrated and angry at the way Mr. Bill changed the rules any time he felt sorry for someone. What really made Carrie mad was that Mr. Bill seemed to think nothing of putting them into impossible situations. This kind of thing had happened before—Mr. Bill would offer help to some needy person and it would be up to Pete and Carrie to make it happen. Carrie felt that, by continuing to bail out Mr. Bill, they were acting as enablers for his bad habits. Pete pointed out that they were sort of forced into this situation since it was Mr. Bill who had started the ministry and besides, he provided most of the money. He was an amazing fund-raiser and had many loyal supporters who gave generously to the project.

Eventually they calmed down and then spent a long time reviewing the vision and goals for this ministry. They discussed the problems of trying to do two kinds of ministry at once—trying to help people get on their feet and established, while at the same time having an "open door" policy for anyone who just needed a place to sleep for one or two nights. Once again, they realized that it was impossible to do both—at least if they wanted to do it well.

The next morning Pete phoned Mr. Bill again and asked him to come out and settle the issue with Francisca. He arrived early in the afternoon and was greeted like a rock star. The kids who had been playing in the back courtyard heard the distinctive sound of his SUV engine and came running in the back door of the café, greeting their hero and begging him to come out and play with them. By the time he got out to the playground, Mr. Bill had kids hanging all over him. At the playground he pushed kids on the swings, lifted up the little ones to the monkey bars, and ran through the obstacle course with the bigger boys.

Carrie was in the kitchen, preparing coffee and watching the scene out back. It irritated her that the kids were so happy to play with Mr. Bill but paid little attention to Pete who had organized the men at the Refuge to create the playground. They had done a terrific job using salvaged lumber and old tires, and even a cargo net that someone found on the beach. It occurred to Carrie that Pete was the one who was always there to enforce the rules and keep the kids in line, so no wonder Mr. Bill was more popular whenever he showed up.

The women living at the Refuge also lined up to talk with Mr. Bill, to ask for favors or advice, all of which took a long time. Eventually he had a chance to talk with Francisca. He told her that he would try to get reservations for her and her children to take the bus to Lima where there were people who might be able to help her further. Francisca thanked him, and wiped away a tear.

Carrie took a deep breath; the next thing on the agenda was for her and Pete to have an honest talk with Mr. Bill and let him know how frustrated they were. She hoped they could do so in a calm, civilized manner. It would not do for their guests to hear the missionaries having an angry argument!

She started to pour coffee and thought it looked peculiar; how many scoops had she put in? She had been distracted by her thoughts and suspected she had made the coffee way too strong. Well, there was no time to make more; hopefully, it wasn't impossible to drink. She filled the cups and brought them to the table where Pete and Mr. Bill were just sitting down.

Pete opened the discussion, sharing the ideas he and Carrie had talked about the night before. He reminded Mr. Bill that the original vision involved working long-term with people, helping them get their lives together and hopefully discipling them. Bringing in people like Francisca just complicated things and distracted them from their primary goal. Mr. Bill replied, agreeing with Pete's assessment, but adding that it just broke his heart to see so many needy people and do nothing to help them. Carrie sat silent while the two men kept saying the same things over and over. The discussion reminded her of a ping pong game where the ball went back and forth but no one scored any points.

Finally, Pete broke the impasse with the suggestion that Mr. Bill should avoid the downtown plaza where the Venezuelans congregated, not going there unless he knew there was room at the Refuge to take in a new family.

Mr. Bill was shocked at the suggestion. "But that's my life," he exclaimed, "working with people. I love going to the plaza and talking with people. They are so open! These people are really in need and they are ready to listen to the gospel. But I can't just preach—I have to show compassion, too. Don't you remember I John 3:17? 'If anyone has material possessions and sees his brother in need but has no pity on him, how can the love of God be in him?'"

Pete said nothing; it was hard to argue against Scripture.

After an uncomfortable silence that seemed to last for several minutes, Carrie decided to jump into the discussion. She hoped that she could speak calmly and without rancor. "Perhaps it would help if we look at the Refuge as a family," she suggested. "Doesn't it seem irresponsible to keep having more babies if you can't take care of the kids you already have?"

Mr. Bill rocked back in his chair, almost tipping over. A minute went by before he stood up and said, "I guess you have a point." With that, he walked out to his SUV. Pete watched him through the open door and noticed that there was no spring in his step. Carrie cleared the table and dumped three cups of cold coffee into the sink.

That night Pete and Carrie had another long discussion about the situation. They believed that the ministry of Casa de Refugio was strategic;

helping people get established in the community and discipling them was the path that would lead to planting a church in this impoverished neighborhood. What they were doing reminded Pete of something he had heard about the difference between giving someone a fish and teaching him how to fish. He strongly believed in the importance of teaching people how to fish.

At the same time, he admitted that Mr. Bill actually had an important role as a gifted evangelist. A number of their guests had become believers as a result of Mr. Bill's ministry. In the end Pete and Carrie agreed that they needed to work together with Mr. Bill, but it was so hard, with their different personalities and gifts.

The next day Francisca was still with them, waiting to hear from don Guillermo. She offered to help with some gardening and Pete paid her enough to buy food for her family.

In the afternoon Pete's phone rang; it was Mr. Bill, asking if they would like to go out for dinner. Pete wasn't sure where this was going, but he agreed to the idea. Mr. Bill and his wife, a lovely Peruvian lady, picked them up just after sunset and drove to a nice restaurant on the touristy side of the beach. During dinner nothing was said about the previous day's conversation, but it was on everyone's mind.

Finally, while waiting for their dessert, Pete asked Mr. Bill what he was going to do about Francisca. That cleared the way for an open discussion. First Mr. Bill apologized for his personality failings that had caused so much trouble. He realized he was just too soft-hearted sometimes and ended up making things difficult for Pete and Carrie. His desire to help people caused him to forget the guidelines he himself had set up for the ministry. He promised to do better in the future.

Pete and Carrie accepted his apology and told him that his gift as an evangelist was really an important part of the ministry. In the end, they all agreed that they needed each other, and promised that they would try to do a better job of communicating. Mr. Bill said he had thought about Carrie's comment on taking care of the kids you already have. It made sense and he would try to follow through on that idea. As far as Francisca was concerned, he had made bus reservations for her and would take her and her kids to the station tomorrow afternoon.

When they parted, Pete and Carrie opted to walk home; it was less than two miles along the beach and then a few blocks through their neighborhood. The evening breeze was pleasant, and they had a lot to talk about. They were cautiously optimistic about how things would work in the future; they knew that Mr. Bill was agreeing with them in his head, but his heart might take him in a different direction. They would have to proceed carefully. Having regular team meetings with Mr. Bill might help keep them all on the same page.

The next morning, after a good night's sleep, Pete was feeling energized as he led devotions. He was delighted that a number of the Venezuelans participated and shared some good insights. Francisca was glad to learn that Mr. Bill had made bus reservations and would come to pick up her and the kids in the afternoon.

When Mr. Bill arrived around three o'clock, everyone was happy to see him, including Pete and Carrie. Francisca's belongings were loaded into the SUV and then all the Venezuelan ladies crowded around to say good-bye to her. Francisca hugged both Isabella and Carrie and thanked them for the time of rest they had provided and for the nice religious words. She asked Pete and Carrie to say prayers for her as she traveled on to Chile.

Observations

Studies of missionary attrition indicate that the most common reason for missionaries leaving the field is the inability to get along with other missionaries. This will seem shocking to people who put missionaries on a pedestal, assuming they have achieved a high level of maturity and spirituality. The truth is missionaries are just like everybody else. They have personalities that may clash with each other. Their gifts may not mesh. They come with their own worldview and may not even be aware that fellow workers tend to see things differently. They may spring from different cultures, either their national culture or their generational culture.

Beyond basic mind-set issues, there are other sources of conflict, including hierarchy—who is the boss? In secular business there is a boss with a chain of command under him. People know their place in the organization. With a mission team it may not be obvious who is in charge, and who makes decisions. Sometimes it may be a matter of seniority; the person who has been there the longest and has the most experience is seen as the leader of the group. Or the person who has invested the most money and time in the project may be considered the boss.

Another possibility is that a person with a strong personality and a take-charge attitude will assume leadership, whether other people like it or not.

Missionaries who are loners, or stubborn, are not unheard of. In fact, in pioneer settings those character qualities may be an asset. Nationals have explained to me how beneficial an older missionary's "holy stubbornness" was for the church in the early days. But, as time goes on and others come to join the work, the pioneer may become a cantankerous old man who impedes progress.

Personality conflicts and leadership issues are common in the local church as well as on the mission field, but the difficulties and fall-out are often worse on the mission field for a number of reasons. Things like climate and local culture can stress the workers, leaving them with little emotional reserves. There may be the sense of living in a fishbowl, with nationals watching every move the missionary makes. Having a very small group of expats with whom one can relate can be difficult. In the home country a person can choose his friends, and find those he can click with, but on the mission field he may be stuck with a group of people, none of whom would be his choice for a good friend.

Conflict is not all bad. Learning to get along with people who differ from us has been called "God's sandpaper" which He uses to smooth our rough edges. Conflict can bring maturity and develop character traits like flexibility, patience, understanding, love, and especially humility. Biblically, we are encouraged to rejoice in trials, but we don't always think of our missionary colleagues in that category. In addition to rejoicing in trials, we can rejoice that as Christians we are uniquely equipped to solve interpersonal problems with forgiveness and love.

Questions

1. What factors can you think of that would cause missionaries to have trouble in getting along with each other?

2. Sources of conflict may not be obvious in the beginning and may blindside a new missionary. How can he or she prepare for unexpected disagreements?

3. If you were a leader in the commending church of either Pete or Mr. Bill, how might you encourage them to resolve their conflict?

9

Choices: Married or Single?
Independent or Mission Board?

Pete and Carrie had moved to a rental house just outside Chiclayo, and now they were looking forward to their first over-night guest, their old friend, Alex. After a year and a half of living in the tiny upstairs apartment at Casa de Refugio, they were enjoying having some extra space. Not a lot of space, really—most of the time the guest room functioned as their office. And when the futon was unfolded to make a bed, it almost filled the whole room.

Having extra space was a plus, but what was really appealing was having some much-needed separation from the ministry at the Refuge. Being on call "twenty-four seven" had begun to take a toll on them. It was a help to be able to pull back a bit physically, as they actually had more responsibility now. Mr. Bill had obtained property for a second Casa de Refugio and had enlisted a young Peruvian couple to oversee it. Pete and Carrie were training them as well as keeping things functioning at the original Refuge.

Just before they moved to the new place they received several unexpected large gifts on their monthly statement from the mission service organization. This enabled them to buy some nice furniture, including the futon, and enough matching dishes and extra chairs to have a group over for a meal. Carrie had put a lot of effort into furnishing and decorating, and now she was looking forward to having guests. The rumble of a motorcycle engine outside told her that Alex had arrived, so she quickly phoned Pete and told him to come home. She and Pete were both looking forward to some serious debriefing, finding out what Alex had been up to since his move to Moyobamba.

Pete arrived home just as Alex finished unloading his gear and stowing it in the guest room. Carrie had prepared a pitcher of ice cold lemonade and they all sat down at the kitchen table for a cool drink and a long talk. Pete had a number of things he wanted to ask Alex about, but he quickly realized that, after the long lonely trip, Alex needed to unwind by reviewing his travels, and Pete's questions would have to wait. Neither Pete nor Carrie could get a word in edgewise as Alex described the scenery and road conditions along the way, aided by an amazing number of pictures on his phone.

Technically, Alex had traveled *down* from Moyobamba to Chiclayo, from an elevation of 2800 feet to sea level, but there were lots of ups as well as downs as he crossed ridges in the Andes Mountains. Moyobamba is on the eastern slope of the Andes where the mountains give way to the jungle, so the first day of traveling was the toughest with constant ups and downs over very high terrain. Wisely, Alex stopped overnight at a town called Pedro Ruis and finished the trip the following day. His pictures were great— vertical cliffs giving way to flat, fertile valleys; deep gorges with rivers running at the bottom; a zigzag footpath up a steep hillside with a heavily loaded donkey and his master trudging along. And, of course, there were numerous pictures featuring the 600 Kawasaki in the foreground with some gorgeous scene behind it. By the time Alex approached the coast, he was done taking pictures, with the scenery fading into gray flatness, dusty fields, and piles of garbage along the road.

When the travelogue was finished, Carrie began preparing dinner while Alex showered and erased the road grime. Soon they were seated at the table, enjoying a delicious meal and reminiscing about their youthful adventures in missions. When Carrie served dessert for the three of them and coffee for her and Alex, Pete figured it was time for his questions about what Alex had been doing since he changed gears and became the in-country representative for Teen Treks.

Alex launched into an explanation of his current activities, starting with his one room apartment in Moyobamba. After several years of recruiting and leading mission teams from a base in the States, the leadership of Teen Treks had asked him to organize their work in Peru. Basically, his job was to coordinate with local churches that wanted to host a work team, figure out the scope of the project they were interested in, check on availability of supplies, and make sure living accommodations were available for each team. When the teams arrived from the States, he handled their care from the time they flew into Lima until they left and went home. Last season he had supervised five teams, taking them to different churches and communities that had volunteered to host them.

The other part of Alex's ministry was to find Peruvian Christian translators to work with the teams, as well as training believers in various churches in how to do evangelism. The local believers would learn the same evangelism techniques that the visitors from the States were using and would be able to come alongside and help the visitors share the gospel when they did VBS or street evangelism. It was a great package: the gringos would attract a lot of attention in the community and would generate enthusiasm among the Peruvian believers. The hope was that the Peruvians would be inspired to continue evangelistic outreaches after the team went back to the States.

Pete was intrigued by some of Alex's training lingo. The concepts were biblical, but there were a lot of new terms being used, some being attempts at redefining old truths. Alex talked about a "house of peace", "missional purpose", "seekers" and other cutting-edge phrases. Pete wondered how some of these terms would translate into Spanish, but then he realized that the ideas were recognizable from Jesus' teaching to the twelve disciples, and then to the seventy that He sent out. However, the way Alex explained everything seemed like a rigid and prescribed process, with not too much thinking for oneself or letting the Holy Spirit guide. Pete checked himself, thinking that he was getting a bit judgmental.

Alex went on to explain his vision for the future. He was hoping to visit communities in San Martin province and out into the Amazon River system as well. He knew that teams from the States would be fascinated to visit the jungle and preach the gospel to the "savages". It sounded so cutting edge, or maybe the edge of the world.

The next morning Pete and Carrie gave Alex a tour of the ministry at Casa de Refugio. On arrival they got a royal welcome—one of the perks of not living on the property. Alex immediately jumped into kicking a soccer ball around with the kids and was a big hit. Carrie checked on the ladies working in the bakery, making sure they had enough flour and other ingredients. Eventually Pete pulled everyone together for morning devotions. It was primarily a group of kids who gathered, as most of the men and some of the women had gone out to work. Pete and Alex decided to do an impromptu Bible story skit, which the kids loved. Afterward Pete and Carrie showed Alex the bakery, explaining that several women baked rolls each morning and then the older kids went out to sell them on the street. The project brought in some needed funds and was a good training venture for the people involved. So far, Carrie was serving as bookkeeper for the bakery, but was teaching one of the older women to handle that task. One of the Venezuelan women had taken over management of the coffee shop and seemed to be doing a good job of supervising the former street boys who helped out in the afternoons.

Alex was impressed at how well the Refuge project was going, and that some of the people had gotten far enough ahead to move out. There was actually a vacancy, and Mr. Bill was in the process of selecting another needy family to move in. The morning passed quickly, and then Pete suggested going to the Chiclayo Mall for lunch at TGIFriday.

The Mall was amazing to Alex—there was even a Starbucks; certainly up-scale from anything available in Moyobamba. They were a little ahead of the 2:00 crowd, so the place was quiet and perfect for visiting. While waiting for their food, Carrie started in on Alex about when he was going to settle down and find a wife. Alex took the teasing well and danced around the idea for a while. Finally, he got serious and gave a straight answer. Marriage seemed unlikely, with his busy schedule that involved a lot of traveling. He figured no woman would want a life like his. Also, there was the financial side of things. Before moving overseas, he had to raise a certain amount of support, and it was hard to reach the quota. If he got married, the required amount would go up farther, according to the mission guidelines. As it was, the mission was urging him to shore up his support which had dropped below 85%.

Carrie and Pete exchanged a knowing look. Pete reminded Alex of the advantages of being simply commended by their home assembly, with no one prescribing what their income should be. He and Carrie were thankful for the organization that processed funds for them, but made no effort to direct their activities, believing that was the prerogative of the commending church. With no minimum support level, they could testify of God's provision for them through some low times, as well as better times financially.

They had learned some practical things along the way, particularly in the area of corresponding with their supporters. They made it a priority to write to donors each month, to thank them for the gifts that were sent. Actually, they sent out e-mails to a large group of interested Christians, adding a personal note to those whom they were thanking for contributions. Early on they included pictures with these monthly updates, but as time went on and the novelty wore off, it was harder to remember to take pictures. The letter writing took a chunk of time out of their busy life, but both Pete and Carrie were convinced that it was important to communicate with friends and especially to send prayer requests. Actually, sending prayer requests was fairly easy; the harder part was remembering to let people know when prayers had been answered.

Pete admitted that writing regular letters was not a magic bullet. Their monthly support was random at best. In the early days they had to dip into savings that they had accumulated before coming to Peru. Most of the time now they had enough to cover the needs of the month, and once in a while they received larger surprise gifts—for instance, the recent gifts that enabled them to furnish the new house. The whole finance thing was a bit mysterious, but exciting and reassuring when you let God provide for you.

Alex countered with the comment that his mission board made sure that its workers budgeted for a house, a vehicle and insurance. Pete admitted that for him and Carrie, the insurance question was a problem. They had had discussions about it, debating what to do, especially in regard to medical insurance. They had talked about various options including Peruvian medical insurance, and a savings account to cover out-of-pocket expenses. So far, they hadn't come up with a good solution.

Over the few days that Alex stayed with them they enjoyed sharing the differences and similarities in their ministries. Pete and Carrie were surprised to learn that Alex, too, had some difficulties with people on his team. Sometimes demands were made from leaders in the US that did not make sense in the country, but when Alex questioned these ideas, his suggestions were rebuffed. He admitted to feeling frustrated but needed to trust the Lord to work out problems and see these situations as an opportunity to learn humility and forgiveness.

Soon Alex was ready to be on his way, driving south to Lima to get paperwork started for a residency permit. From there he planned to drive up over the mountains to Huanuco, then north along the eastern edge of the Andes to Tarapoto and finally, back home to Moyobamba. It was a pretty ambitious trip, covering almost 1900 kilometers (1180 miles). Pete and Carrie hoped things would go smoothly and that he would find friends to stay with along the way.

Observations

Single vs. Married: Alex's single lifestyle allows him a lot of freedom, but he also has to deal with loneliness. He may have more time to devote to mission work, but he lacks someone to help with the chores of daily life. Without a partner to strategize with and discuss plans, he may pursue impractical goals.

It should be noted that a single missionary may not have deliberately chosen that path. Many would like to be married, but never found the right person, someone with the same desire to serve the Lord. A well-known missionary from the last century was Gladys Alyward who served in China. She felt strongly that she needed a husband to partner with her and asked the Lord to send someone. When no husband ever showed up, she decided that it wasn't the Lord's fault; He had called someone, but the man didn't accept the call.

The married missionary faces different challenges from the single worker. He needs to consider the needs of his family which may sometimes limit his effectiveness in ministry. However, his family is an important part of his ministry. Watching the interactions of the missionary family, people learn how a Christian family operates. Nationals may have greater appreciation for a married missionary, seeing him as more mature, even if he is younger than his single colleague.

Mission board vs. Independent: The mission board approach has some attractive features. It is sort of like a packaged tour; things are planned and organized so there are fewer opportunities to make mistakes. There is security, with provisions for insurance and retirement. There may be training for dealing with emergencies, such as terror attacks. The mission may insist that its workers return home if a dangerous situation develops. Play it safe, avoid risks. In major decisions, the mission board makes the call, not the individual missionary.

The independent missionary has a lot more freedom to make his own decisions—and maybe make some mistakes. There is certain exhilaration in following this path, looking to the Lord for guidance, plus getting advice from trusted people in the commending church. The missionary has the joy of walking by faith and looking to God for his needs. Some may see him as foolhardy, but I believe God will honor the person who steps out in faith.

Another theme in this chapter relates to communication with supporters. I personally stand by the advice given by Pete and Carrie to write regularly to your supporters. This is essential whether you are an independent missionary or are working under a mission board. It is important to keep people informed, and acknowledge gifts received. Nowadays there are multiple ways of keeping in touch, but somehow missionaries still struggle with this task. When I was growing up my parents communicated by airmail and I helped by licking envelopes. I can still remember the funny taste in my mouth after licking forty or more. Sometimes my dad would include pictures and it was tricky to use some silkscreen process to get a sharp black and white image.

Then e-mail came along—much cheaper and faster than airmail. And now we have all kinds of choices including FaceBook, Twitter and blogs. Posting monthly updates to a blog has been my preferred method of communicating. With all of these choices available, it becomes a matter of knowing what your audience responds to. Different platforms reach different people. FaceBook has become the favorite of 50+ age people who like to look at pictures and make comments. Twitter is more of a business mindset so you often hit the 40+ crowd; links are noted, but not necessarily read. Younger people seem to prefer text messages. Missionaries need not be on the cutting edge of communication technology, but they do have something important to say and should keep up with the times. With all these options and more, the media can take over your life if you aren't careful. And that is not just for missionaries, it is a problem for almost everyone.

Questions

1. Concerning the question of marriage vs. single, which do you think would be most effective for ministry in the long run, and in the short run?

2. Compare advantages and disadvantages of working under a mission board vs. being independent.

3. Why is it so important to thank people for financial gifts, when it is actually to the Lord that they are giving?

4. Some missionaries have made it a point to never express their financial needs to anyone except the Lord. Others are quite open about their needs, even telling exactly how much money they need for a certain project. If you were a missionary, what path would you follow in this area?

Jesse Mattix & Peggy Covert

10

Furlough

Following her mother-in-law into Sam's Club, Carrie felt a twinge of disappointment. For weeks, as she and Pete counted down to furlough, this was a big item on her to-do list. She wasn't actually planning on buying anything today, but it was fun to look around and see everything in the huge store. The problem was that now, instead of the excitement she expected, she just felt tired.

She had to admit that she had reason to be tired. The last few weeks had been intense, as she and Pete deep-cleaned their apartment and stashed away personal belongings so one of the Venezuelan families could live there. The trip from Chiclayo to Lima was long—12 hours on a bus—in order to save $400 each on plane tickets. Arriving at the Lima airport they found the usual madhouse at check-in; endless lines snaking back and forth, and people with huge boxes and suitcases piled precariously on carts. They finally got their boarding passes and then looked at the reader board which listed their midnight flight as scheduled for 2:15 a.m.

The only place to sit for the next few hours was the busy food court. Eventually they were allowed to proceed to the departure lounge where they sat for two hours more. Their plane pushed back right at 2:15, but then sat on the tarmac for another half hour before finally taking off. As soon as possible the flight attendants served meals, but at that hour all Carrie wanted to do was sleep. Pete was happy to eat her meal, as well as his own.

Arriving at LAX only two hours late, they trudged through the routine of passport control and customs, listening to announcements in both English and Spanish. A stop at the restroom was almost mind-blowing; the place was so clean and classy, and there was hot water and the electric hand-dryers actually worked. At the passenger pick-up area Pete's parents were waiting for them; it felt good to collapse in the backseat and not have to think about what to do next. Soon they were on the freeway, and amazed at the orderliness of the traffic, buzzing along at something over the official speed limit. In Peruvian cities traffic was slow and chaotic; a road marked for three lanes would often have five cars abreast, plus motor scooters sneaking through in between. Here, people seemed to pretty much follow the rules; on the surface streets, they were startled to see cars stopping for pedestrians. Quite a change from the every-man-for-himself mindset they had become used to.

Pete's parents took them to the missionary guest house where they would be staying for the next few months. It was such a blessing to have a furnished home to live in. The house had belonged to an elderly lady, known to everyone as Miss Lillian. In her will she left the house to the chapel with the stipulation that it be used to provide a restful refuge for tired missionaries. Walking into the house, Carrie was touched, almost to the point of tears, at how nice everything was. There was even a bouquet of fresh flowers on the dining table. Pete checked out the well-stocked fridge and discovered two cases of Dr. Pepper! There was a casserole that only needed to be heated in the microwave, and a beautiful fruit salad, plus a chocolate cake for dessert. Knowing it was way more than two people could eat, Carrie asked Pete's parents to stay for dinner. They had a good time together, catching up on family and church news. By the time dinner was over, Carrie really looked bushed, so her mother-in-law insisted on cleaning up the kitchen and advised Pete and Carrie to go to bed, even though it wasn't dark yet.

Saturday turned out to be a busy, but pleasant day. After a leisurely breakfast, they finished unpacking their bags, in between answering the phone. A number of friends knew they had arrived and wanted to drop by for a short visit. They ended up with one group leaving as the next group arrived and it went on like that all day. Most of the visitors brought some kind of welcome home gift, or a snack, so it was easy to be hospitable, and they ended up snacking most of the day. In the evening Pete spent some time preparing a short report to present during the Sunday morning church service.

Sunday turned out to be enjoyable, but not really relaxing. It was nice to live just a few blocks from the chapel, so they could walk there. Later in the week, Carrie's dad and one of her sisters would be driving down from Santa Barbara with a car to lend them. Before and after the services, there were so many people to talk to, and a number of them were anxious to have Pete and Carrie over for a meal. Between them, they managed to accept two invitations for lunch and had to ask one of the families if it would be okay to come for supper instead. They ended up with a very busy day, and too much to eat.

No wonder Carrie felt tired on Monday as she roamed the aisles of Sam's Club, dazzled by the overwhelming variety of things to buy. She reveled in the feeling of freedom—store clerks did not hover over the customers and shoppers tended to spread out, not crowding each other. Eventually, having seen just about everything in the store, Carrie and her mother-in-law returned to the car to meet Pete and his dad, who showed up twenty minutes late. The guys had been having such a great time at Tool Town, that it was hard to pull themselves away.

Next stop was lunch and Pete's dad suggested either Porky Pizza or Rubio's Coastal Grill. Pete knew his folks would prefer the Grill which featured seafood, but he and Carrie were craving real American pizza. They could get ceviche and other fish anytime in Peru, but pizza was another matter. Peruvian pizza was a dry affair with very little cheese or even sauce, sparingly arranged on a pre-cooked crust. No wonder it wasn't considered a meal, just a snack. Another factor in favor of eating at Porky Pizza was…free refills on Dr. Pepper. Pete drank three large glasses and needed a stop at the restroom before they headed home.

When Pete's parents dropped them off, Carrie was ready for a nap. While she slept Pete worked on plans for the near future and discovered that almost nothing was planned. They would go to the midweek meeting at the chapel on Wednesday, and then the elders and deacons had invited both of them to a special debriefing on Thursday evening. Other than that, Pete had nothing on his Day-Timer, and it seemed kind of strange.

Pete spent the next couple of hours on the phone, talking to friends from various nearby assemblies, checking out the possibility of visiting and giving a report about the work in Peru. Being used to the spontaneity of Peruvian planning (or non-planning), he hadn't realized that he should have contacted these people a month ago to get on their schedule. Most were gracious and invited him to come early next month, either on Sunday morning or Wednesday night. The smaller assemblies were glad to have someone to provide teaching, so that would require developing some messages that he could share. By the time Carrie woke from her nap, Pete was feeling slightly depressed, wondering how he would cope with several months of inactivity. The long-awaited furlough suddenly seems a bit like a jail sentence.

"Times have changed," Pete mused. He remembered Mr. Edney telling him how things were when he was growing up in the 1950's when a missionary could schedule a meeting just about any night of the week, and lots of people would attend. Of course, things were different back then, with not as many diversions. Most Christians hadn't succumbed to the lure of a TV set, and there were few sporting events, other than professional baseball. A missionary showing color slides was big entertainment in a lot of places, and if he was a good storyteller and could display an eighteen-foot long snake skin, or demonstrate the use of a blow-gun, so much the better.

Thursday evening Pete and Carrie made a point of arriving a few minutes early for the meeting with the deacons and elders. In Peru they would have timed their arrival a bit on the late side, but this was not Peru. Carrie felt a little out of place, being the only woman there, and she determined to say nothing, unless specifically asked. Pete gave an overview of their years in Peru, briefly mentioning language school, and then focusing on the time they had spent at Casa de Refugio. He explained the conflict they had had with Mr. Bill and said that things had been going better lately. Along the way, various people interrupted with questions, some being right to the point, and others kind of off the wall. Pete thought to himself that he could guess who read his monthly updates and who didn't.

Carrie was a bit taken aback when one of the men asked her to tell specifically what she had been doing during their time in Chiclayo. Taking a moment to gather her thoughts, she began tentatively, but then picked up enthusiasm, talking about developing the bakery project and, more recently, beginning to train one of the women to do the book-keeping. She also mentioned that most afternoons she spent some time tutoring various kids who were behind in their schoolwork.

When she paused for breath, Pete broke in, saying, "In addition to all that, she keeps me well-fed, and having clean clothes to wear." Everyone chuckled and nodded approvingly. Then Dr. Hausenberger, a philosophy professor known for occasional thoughtless remarks, commented, "Vell, ven you have children you vill need to stay at home and not do all these other things."

The silence was deafening. Pete and Carrie could think of nothing to say, but both of them suddenly realized that they had unconsciously subscribed to the notion that was common among people their age: *"Kids? Sure, but not now. Not until we get established in our careers."*

Mr. Fulton, who was chairing the meeting, came to their rescue, noting that Pete and Carrie were still on Peruvian time, three hours ahead of California, so it would be wise to end the meeting soon and let them go home, unless anyone needed to ask one more question.

Mr. Edney, who had been sitting quietly the whole time, spoke up. "Excuse me if I am being too personal, Carrie. My wife and I have noticed that you seem rather pale, not like your usual self. We are afraid you may have picked up some tropical bug and are wondering if you have thought of seeing a doctor."

If anyone else had said that Carrie might have been offended. But Mr. Edney was such an old dear, and she knew he and his wife really cared about them and prayed for them regularly. She swallowed the lump in her throat and thanked him for his thoughtfulness.

As they walked home from the meeting, Pete suggested that Carrie should call their family doctor tomorrow and make an appointment. She agreed, thinking that she had been too tired for too long and it would be good to find out what was going on.

When Carrie talked to the receptionist at the clinic, the first appointment available was two weeks away. Hearing her concerns about tropical bugs, the woman set up the appointment for early morning, telling her to come in fasting—no breakfast—in order to get more accurate blood work.

Pete went with her to the appointment and they planned to stop at McDonalds on the way home and enjoy Eggs McMuffin and everything else on the menu. Arriving at the clinic, they were directed to the lab where Carrie provided the required specimens. Then, on to an examining room where a nurse checked her vitals—height, weight, temperature and blood pressure. Everything looked normal, though Carrie had lost a few pounds compared to her last check-up several years ago.

Doctor James walked in, asked a few questions, and then said he would check the lab results and come back. While they waited, Pete scrolled through articles about tropical diseases on his phone and Carrie flipped through a tattered copy of "Coastal Hideaways" a magazine which featured gorgeous mansions on the Pacific Coast. *"Only in California; nothing like this in Peru,"* Carrie though with amusement.

Eventually the doctor came back with a big smile on his face and assured Carrie that she definitely did not have any type of tropical disease. Before she had a chance to ask what she *did* have, he reached out to Pete and shook his hand, announcing, "Congratulations, Pete. You are going to be a father!" Pete nearly fell off his chair, and Carrie burst into tears.

Realizing that the news was a shock to them, Dr. James rearranged his schedule and spent an unusual amount of time, talking through the situation. He assured them that it would be okay to have the baby in Peru. In fact, a former colleague was director of a clinic in Lima and would be able make a referral for a good Ob-gyn doctor in Chiclayo.

Fortified by the doctor's encouragement, Pete and Carrie left the clinic, still in a bit of a daze. Instead of McDonalds they decided to celebrate their new status by going upscale and having a good breakfast at Waffle World. While they waited for the food to be served, they tried to think of some clever way to announce their big news to family and friends. After breakfast they stopped at a bookstore on the way home and bought several books, including *"What to Expect when You're Expecting"* and a fat little volume that had thousands of the most popular names for babies.

They waited until the next appointment to share the news with everyone. Dr. James assured them that everything was normal and scheduled an ultrasound. Armed with the grainy black and white images, they made the big announcement first to family and then to friends. It was interesting to see the different reactions. Everyone, of course, was delighted to hear the news, but there were opposing views on where the baby should be born, about half voting for USA, and the other half for Peru.

Even their relatives were divided: not surprisingly, Pete's mom and Carrie's sisters were determined that they should stay in California for the delivery. The two prospective grandpas had a more laid-back view. Pete's dad commented that Peru was a civilized country, and healthy babies were born there all the time. Carrie's dad declared that God could take care of this baby in Peru just as well as in the States.

Among their friends, Carrie was most encouraged by Mrs. Edney who told her, "Your baby will be just fine in Peru. When our little Bethany was born, we were living in a jungle house with a dirt floor. I was so thankful when Bethany started walking early, at nine months, and stopped crawling around in the dirt."

Both Pete and Carrie were anxious to get back to Peru. The pregnancy added a new dimension to the furlough, but they still felt like they had too much time on their hands. Dr. James was encouraging about their travel plans, noting that their scheduled departure date would be about halfway through the pregnancy, well within the airline regulations for pregnant passengers. He commented humorously, "Flying that early, you won't need to request a seatbelt extension." He and Pete both thought that was funny. Carrie was not amused.

Observations

Most missionaries have mixed feelings about furloughs. The word seems to imply a vacation or time to relax and that is somewhat true. But often you hover between being crazy busy on weekends and then aimless and bored during the week. For some, the solution is to travel all over the country, visiting many churches and supporters. The missionary's children may enjoy this, or not. Especially tedious for the kids is hearing Dad give the same talk over and over, until they have the whole thing memorized.

Having hosts who take the kids on special outings is a great blessing for the traveling missionary family and gives the MK's a more positive outlook on this time in the "old country". Please don't ask the kids if they are happy to be home; they may actually be homesick for the country they have grown up in, and don't see the USA as home in any sense. They may also be struggling to communicate in English.

One reason for traveling extensively it that it provides somewhere to stay— for a night or two in one location, then off to somewhere else. One missionary mom described her family's furlough as "being gypsies for Jesus". Having a place to stay is a big concern for missionaries on furlough. It is a blessing when the commending assembly assists in some way. In some cities there may be a house or apartments set aside for missionaries. That is a real asset, but it takes some dedicated people to manage the property. Another possibility is renting an apartment or house and furnishing it for the missionary family. One difficulty is that these days missionaries tend to take short furloughs, and it may be hard to find a rental available for less than six months or a year. There are other options, and some can be quite creative, such as renting or borrowing a travel trailer and living in it, parked in someone's driveway. Sometimes a missionary family will be able to live and help out at a Bible Camp.

Next to housing, the biggest concern is often transportation. Friends in the home country can be a big help in this area, and there are a number of ways to do it. Someone might have a car the missionary can borrow or provide one as an outright gift. Sometimes a missionary may have saved up funds to buy a car but would find it helpful if someone scouts out some good possibilities before he arrives, and then takes him shopping. Along with car worries comes insurance and a missionary out of country usually has no record and get the higher insurance rates.

After housing and transportation, probably the next major concern for the missionary on furlough is what to do with his time. Coming from a very busy life on the mission field, and then finding himself with very few responsibilities can be demoralizing. One possibility is to get some kind of job, either for pay or as a volunteer. Besides having something to do, it would provide opportunities to get to know people and have an impact in their lives.

Sometimes well-meaning people try to set the missionary up with tasks that do not fit his abilities, simply because there is a need. For instance, the Bible Camp needs a speaker for junior high week, but the missionary who has recently returned from Outer Ugglstan, hasn't spoken English for five years, and knows nothing about current teen culture is probably not a good choice. Similarly, it is unfair to expect the missionary to arbitrate a long-simmering disagreement among members of the local church. Asking the missionary to teach on the subject of "giving" is very awkward, for obvious reasons!

Ideally, a furlough should be a time of refreshment and reconnecting with the folks at home. The commending assembly can be a big help by planning ahead and asking the missionary some pointed questions: What equipment do you need—car, housing, etc. How would you like to spend your time—a busy schedule of traveling and preaching, or a time of complete rest? Would some kind of continuing education be helpful? What about the children—will they be enrolled in school; would they like to go to summer camp? Many of these topics could be discussed by Skype or WhatsApp before the missionary arrives home.

Once the missionary family has arrived, a welcoming team should go into action. Likely, furnished housing will be ready as well as a vehicle. Often the home church will have a big "welcome" event, but other, smaller events might be helpful. Church families with kids close to the MKs' ages could be encouraged to socialize with the missionary family and plan some activities to help the kids become friends. Boys, especially, can find it hard to make friends and may need some activity to do together to help them "bond". For girls, something like a slumber party or shopping expedition might be welcome. Having a "toy shower" for the MKs might be fun for everyone, especially if the toys are things that a group of kids can enjoy together.

Questions

1. List several important purposes of a furlough.

2. What might be on a missionary's "to do list" as he prepares to leave his mission location for an extended time?

3. How can missionaries prepare their children for furlough?

4. How often should a missionary come home and how long should he stay in the home country?

5. How can the home church help the missionary return to his work refreshed and encouraged?

11

Raising Cross-Cultural Kids

Baby Olivia woke up from her nap, smiling and babbling. She was six months old today, and Carrie had invited friends to a party to celebrate. She realized it might seem strange—why not wait until her first birthday to have a party? But Carrie was thinking of more than Olivia's age; she was thinking of what a difficult and stretching year she had just completed. Actually, it was over a year ago, early in their furlough when they learned about the pregnancy—big surprise! It added a level of complexity to the furlough, and their future plans. They were able to return to Peru on schedule, armed with recommendations for three birthing centers in Chiclayo. They visited all of them and found one that seemed like a good fit.

The last few months of the pregnancy were stressful. It was hot season on the coast and their home had no air conditioning. When they returned from furlough, knowing that their family was growing, they looked for a larger place to live and found a house to rent in the Victoria neighborhood, close to the church they would be attending. Like most houses in the area it had no side yard at all, being built tight up against the houses on each side. There was no front yard, either. Just a one meter set back between the gate on the street and the front door. Moving into a new place involved arranging and rearranging furniture and buying a few new things. It was all a bit much for Carrie, though Pete did most of the work, cleaning and painting their new home and then helping Carrie figure out how to arrange the furniture. Carrie enjoyed setting up the nursery, which had to share space with Pete's office.

Carrie's due-date came...and went, much to her dismay. Waiting was hard enough, but what really stressed her was several friends who phoned every day, sometimes several times a day, wanting to know if she had gone into labor yet.

Finally, after several false alarms and trips to the clinic, Olivia was born early on the morning of February 24, weighing 3.2 kilograms (7lbs. 2 oz.).

For some reason she came into the world angry and screaming. When she continued crying non-stop, the doctor and his assistants finished their work quickly and retreated out of the birthing suite, leaving Carrie and Pete to get acquainted with their firstborn. As soon as the medical people left, Olivia calmed down and looked all around, apparently inspecting her new world. Pete and Carrie were enchanted, gazing at her in awe. Pete whispered, "She's beautiful…just so…so perfect."

Carrie, cuddling the little bundle, was equally thrilled, but commented, "Perfect, yes, but we will probably find out someday that she has a sin nature like everyone else."

In the months that followed, there were endless nights of broken sleep as one or the other of them walked the floor with Olivia who was suffering from colic. The older ladies at church and in the neighborhood were happy to share their remedies for colic and everything else that could afflict a baby. Some of their notions were quite comical. Of course, they all insisted that Olivia needed to be bundled up in a sweater, socks and a hat, plus a blanket. And this during the hottest weather! Carrie tried to be patient, thanking them for their suggestions, but not carrying out most of them.

Around the age of four months the colic subsided and Olivia turned into a happy, delightful baby who loved attention. And that was a good thing, because everyone wanted to visit, and everyone who came wanted to hold, kiss and cuddle her. The visitors continued to give Carrie advice about everything, including getting Olivia's ears pierced as soon as possible. Some suggested shaving her head, which they thought would cause her hair to grow thicker.

As she approached six months, Olivia began sleeping through the night. She had not yet begun teething, so life was pretty calm, causing Carrie to think a party would be in order. She talked it over with her friend, Monica, who helped her with ideas for food, telling her what typical Peruvian party food should be. They would have a cake, of course, but what else? Monica suggested empanadas and "causa" (mashed potato balls dipped in lemon juice). They would also have chips and salsa, along with mashed avocado dip.

The party was scheduled for two o'clock on Saturday afternoon. That was usually Olivia's best time of day, after her morning nap and before she got tired and cranky in the late afternoon. While Olivia was napping Carrie tidied the living room and blew up some balloons and taped them to the walls. Then she arranged pink crepe paper streamers, looping them over the light fixture above the table where the cake was displayed. Pete had gone out to get some bottles of soda. He had hoped to find a few cans of Dr. Pepper, but the best he could come up with was Coke and Inca Cola. He knew that most people would offer some cheap knock-off brand if they were serving a lot of guests, but Pete wanted this party, celebrating his daughter, to be the best he could make it.

Unfortunately, he had been unable to track down one thing Carrie really wanted—a pink candle in the shape of the number six. He reported to Carrie that he had looked all over at the cake store and didn't see any candles. Carrie rolled her eyes and told him that you don't buy candles at the cake shop; you get them at the ice cream store. Then it was Pete's turn to roll his eyes. He offered to go out once more and try to get a candle, but it was already after two o'clock, so they decided to skip it.

By three o'clock, none of the guests had shown up, and Pete was thinking he should have gone out to look for that special candle. Carrie had Olivia dressed in her cutest outfit and was trying to make sure she would stay happy for the party, which should have started a while ago. Finally, there was a knock on the door; Monica had arrived with some candy for the party. She left, saying she would be back soon with Diego and their little boy, Tomas.

Soon other guests began to arrive. Carrie suspected that Monica had made some phone calls to remind people that the party was on. By 4:00 the house was packed with friends, and maybe a few people that Carrie didn't remember inviting. Some of the guests brought gifts—completely unexpected, but very thoughtful of them. They were mostly beautifully wrapped, and Carrie was curious to learn what was inside each one.

Olivia was the center of attention, as just about everyone waited for a chance to hold her. Thankfully, her good mood continued, and she was enjoying her status as the party girl. Carrie was wondered why no one helped themselves to the refreshments on the dining table, but everyone seemed happy, just visiting and playing with Olivia.

Eventually, the inevitable happened; both Olivia and the woman who was holding her just then looked distressed, and someone commented about the bad smell. Carrie, feeling embarrassed, picked up her daughter and rushed to the nursery where she found that Olivia had done quite a job, and needed a complete change of clothing. It took a while to get the baby cleaned up and presentable, and when Carrie rejoined the party, she was relieved to see that Monica and her sister, Nora, had taken over hostess duties.

Monica was giving each guest a small plastic plate loaded with a variety of the snacks available while Nora was handing out plastic cups of either Coke or Inca Cola. It seemed strange to Carrie that people didn't get to serve themselves and choose what they wanted, but she was thankful that Monica and Nora were taking care of the guests.

For Carrie, it seemed like the perfect time to open the gifts. She picked up one—nicely wrapped, with a pink bow on top—and opened it, finding a package of Zwieback cookies. This particular treat was unfamiliar to Carrie, so someone explained that these were special teething cookies, something like biscotti for babies. The next three gifts were all on the same theme—some kind of teething toy—and everyone thought it was funny, especially since Olivia didn't have any teeth yet. Carrie noticed that the givers of the various gifts seemed kind of embarrassed and wondered if she was doing the wrong thing by opening the gifts in front of everyone. Only one gift was left now, and Carrie figured that she better open it. Beautifully wrapped in sparkly paper, this gift proved to be a package of baby wipes. That elicited a lot of laughter as people commented that she should have opened that one earlier. Carrie felt embarrassed and completely at a loss as to what to do next.

Monica came to her rescue, saying that it was time to serve the cake. As Carrie cut the cake, Monica and Nora deftly slid pieces onto plastic plates and served them to the guests. Some people wanted their cake on a napkin, to take home, and a few asked for another piece for someone at home. By the time the last piece was cut, people were heading out the door and Carrie realized the party was over.

Olivia, sensing that she was no longer the center of attention, launched into her normal late afternoon fussiness. Monica urged Carrie to put the baby to bed, saying that she would help Pete clean up while Olivia was getting settled. Olivia was definitely over stimulated, and it took almost twenty minutes of rocking her in a dark, quiet room before she calmed down and slept.

When Carrie returned to the scene of the party, Monica was finishing cleaning up the kitchen and Pete was getting their bedroom back into shape. Some of the kids had made themselves at home there and had left scraps of food and empty plastic cups all over the place, including on the bed. Pete saw that someone had turned on his computer and, from the tabs that were open, he knew they had enjoyed some video games and looked at a couple of things on YouTube. *"These kids are pretty savvy,"* Pete thought to himself, *"but not too well behaved."*

Carrie was surprised that Monica's husband and son had left already. Monica explained that Diego had promised to take Tomas out for ice cream if he behaved well at the party and didn't scream even once. Carrie knew about Tomas's reputation for screaming and other bad behavior. People jokingly called him "Tommy el Terremoto" *(earthquake—slang term for a bratty kid).*

In addition to cleaning up the remains of the party, Monica had made a pot of coffee. She and Carrie sat down at the kitchen table to savor both the coffee and the quiet atmosphere. Monica began talking about her struggles with Tommy, who constantly embarrassed her with his bad behavior, especially when they were out in public. Lately she was having difficulty with him at home, too. If something didn't please him, he would just scream until she relented and gave in to his demands.

Carrie asked if they had ever spanked Tommy and was surprised at the embarrassed look on Monica's face. "My husband lost it once," she admitted, "and used a belt on him. I told him that never again would that be allowed in our house." Monica went on to say that Tommy behaves much better when his dad is home, but she still does not want any more spanking. She added that she was very apprehensive, thinking of sending Tommy to kindergarten next year. Just then Diego returned with a very grumpy looking Tommy. Diego didn't give any explanation, just told Monica that they needed to go home and put Tommy to bed.

After they left Pete and Carrie relaxed in the living room and talked about the party. Some things were a mystery to them, like why people didn't help themselves to the refreshments and why everyone cleared out so quickly after the cake was served. One thing was not a mystery: they did not want Olivia to be a *terremoto* like Tommy, or to be careless of other people's belongings like the kids who had invaded and trashed their bedroom. They agreed that they did not have all the answers, and that they needed to put a lot of thought and prayer into figuring out how to raise their daughter. They also started thinking about ways they could help, in a gracious way, other young parents like Diego and Monica who were struggling with aspects of child-rearing.

Observations

Next to learning a new language, understanding a new culture may be the biggest hurdle a neophyte missionary faces. Actually, culture is trickier than language, since it is not as obvious. If the missionary has come to a culture that looks like his own (rather than to an Indigenous jungle tribe, for instance) he may assume that the local people think like he does. In time, he will begin to notice differences in the ways people interact and think.

As the missionary begins to understand the customs of his new culture, he tries to fit in, but may also feel compelled to be polite by the standards of his home culture. This can cause some interesting conflicts. A classic example involves the concept of time in the Latin world. The missionary will eventually figure out that if he is invited to an event at two o'clock, he should arrive no earlier than three o'clock. Even then, he will be on the early side and will have to wait for things to happen. In his gringo heart, he feels uncomfortable at the thought of arriving late, but knows that if he arrives at the appointed hour—as he would in his home culture—he will be sitting around, doing nothing for long time.

After several years in Peru, Pete and Carrie are just beginning to figure out this part of the culture. They are also learning that you don't serve buffet style at a party. If Monica and Nora had not come to the rescue and done things properly (serving the guests individually), Carrie might have seen the first few guests load up their plates, leaving almost nothing for those coming behind them. Cutting the cake is another cultural difference. For some reason, serving cake is the hint that the party is over, and it is time to go home.

Eventually, by trial and error, the missionary learns the unwritten rules and adapts to the culture—or doesn't adapt, as the case may be. Sometimes an older missionary will revert to being himself, following the rules of his home culture, and people just learn to accept him as he is. Meanwhile, the young missionary is trying hard to understand the culture and fit in, but he needs to realize that in some ways he will never be one of the natives. Balance is needed, as is wisdom. It helps if the missionary has one or more friends in the culture to help guide him.

Child rearing is another cultural mine field, particularly when dealing with other people's children. While cultures do tend to raise children in community, different parts of the community have different contributions they are expected to make. Uncles or older brothers may have a certain role, and teachers, neighbors or family friends have other roles. How the missionary fits in can be hard to figure out. Having a relationship is essential. The closer your relationship with a family, the more input of some kind you are expected to have.

Sometimes the missionary, especially the male variety, will unwittingly be cast in the role of "bad cop". Mothers may scare their children into behaving properly by warning them that the missionary will punish them if they are bad. Of course, it is rather shocking to find out that you are the bad guy, but if you use the role judiciously, there are advantages to being perceived as an authority figure. Judiciously is the key word here; I have gotten into trouble for slapping a kid's hand in public. The problem was, I didn't know him well. No question that he was acting badly, but I did not have the needed relationship with him to straighten him out. Having a relationship and knowing your role are vital factors.

In our North American culture families tend to be private and we often shy away from probing into another family's troubles. In other cultures, if you have developed a close relationship with a family, they may be very willing to tell you their concerns and ask for advice. No guarantee that they will act on the advice given, but over time you may be able to steer them in a good direction.

Raising your own children on the mission field is both a unique blessing and a challenge. Your family is being watched all the time. While being a role model for other families is a great opportunity to be a Christian testimony, the missionary parents should be sensitive to their children and provide needed privacy for the family. Having boundaries is important, including limits in areas such as time, space, and material goods. The missionary family needs time for "just us" where the parents focus on their kids without being distracted by others. It is helpful if the missionary family has some private space, perhaps a room in the house that is not open to visitors. Dealing with personal belongings can be complex. Often the missionary kids will have nicer toys than the local kids who will want to play with those toys and very likely wreck some things. The family may need to designate certain toys for sharing and other things that are kept out of sight of the neighbors.

Acceptable behavior and speech is an area that can create tension. The missionary family will likely have higher standards than their neighbors, and the children need to learn what is acceptable and what is not. There are stories of missionary kids picking up the local language faster than their parents, and then eventually mom and dad find out the kids are using some very salty language!

Ideally, the missionary wants his children to be "in the world but not of it". The kids can be a great blessing just by being themselves and attracting other children to join in their activities. The missionary family, going about their daily life in full view of the local community, can be a testimony for Christ. In reality, a well-raised family on the mission field can become one of the best tools for ministry.

Questions

1. Cultural adaptation is good and necessary, but can a person go too far? What might be an example of overdoing assimilation?

2. What sources of help or information would you suggest to aid the new missionary in adapting to the culture?

3. What are some areas of culture that a missionary should not adapt to? (Is culture spiritually or morally neutral?)

4. How should a missionary react to his inevitable cultural blunders?

12

Missionary Project

Pete had been standing in line all day. At least, it felt that way. Actually, this was his second time to stand in line at the Sunarp office (government agency for business licenses, tax numbers, etc.). The first time around all he managed to do was learn that he needed to bring several more documents. So now, here he was again, hoping that he had all the right paperwork with him this time. If so, the office would proceed with the requested authorization for the business name he was reserving.

Earlier in the day he had gone to the National Bank to pay some legal fees, and also talked with Jaime, his lawyer friend. Jaime had seemed to know everything when they started this whole process, but now he was just as mystified as Pete as they stumbled through the procedure. The requirements were mind-numbing: every document required certified and legalized copies, stamped by a notary and with proof that fees had been paid for each of them. Pete thought he was making progress, but at every turn there seemed to be a new requirement that everyone had forgotten to mention, or that applied only to foreigners.

As the line inched forward Pete asked himself what he was trying to accomplish, and if it was worth the trouble. It had seemed such a beautiful and simple idea at the beginning: a Christian Youth Center where the local evangelical churches could team up to meet the needs of the city's youth. So many kids were hanging out on the streets, having no place to go. With a majority of families living in small, overcrowded apartments, social life happened on the streets; lots of bad stuff happened on the streets, too. Having a clean, safe, and fun place for kids would be such a blessing. It would be an opportunity for discipleship of Christian kids, and evangelism for the unsaved who would be attracted by the activities offered.

The attractions provided at the Youth Center would include food. Pete had visited similar ministries in other cities and learned that food was key; kids like to eat! Thus, his efforts to meet all the legal requirements included a mountain of paperwork necessary for opening a restaurant. Actually, he wasn't planning a full-blown restaurant, just a snack bar, but the rules were the same. He suspected that no one would ever ask about his food service license, but as a Christian he wanted to do everything in an honorable way.

Pete's cell phone rang. He saw that the call was from Carrie, so he turned and caught the eye of the guy behind him in line, who nodded, indicating that he would save Pete's place. He wanted to talk to his wife, but not at the expense of losing his place in line! Carrie was calling to report that her friend, Monica, was coming over in late afternoon to give them a "head's up" regarding a possible problem with volunteer staffing for the Youth Center, and she thought Pete needed to be there. He calculated the chances of getting home on time and said he would try. He hung up and quickly returned to his place, noting that the line had not moved at all while he was out.

Pete continued reviewing in his mind the process that had brought him to this point. It started out as a dream he and Carrie shared, and then mentioned to a few interested people who turned out to be quite enthusiastic and encouraged them to move ahead with the idea. They knew from the start that money would be an issue; in fact, it would take a miracle to see this dream become reality. They would need to rent or purchase a building, and then there would likely be all kinds of improvements and upgrades required, including kitchen facilities and bathrooms. The wish-list was longer: a large room with a stage, a game room, an office, and practice rooms for various church bands that would perform.

About five months ago a couple of things came together which, looking back, Pete considered to be miracles, or close to it. Carrie's friend, Monica, mentioned a friend of hers whose husband was in the business of developing properties. He was trying to sell a building that just might be what they were looking for. Pete made an appointment to look at the property and found it to be very promising. The location was good, the building was large enough for the activities they were envisioning, and it had a kitchen and one bathroom, both of which would need considerable upgrading. Of course, the sticking point was the price. Even with considerable negotiating, it was pretty steep.

Just at that time Pete got a request from a friend, George Wright, a missionary from one of the large mission organizations who had recently retired and gone back to the States. Pete had gotten to know George through involvement in various projects to help the Venezuelan refugees. The church George had worked with in Chiclayo was preparing to host a work team from the States and needed a translator. George phoned Pete and asked if he could help out. It took some juggling of his schedule, but eventually Pete called George and agreed to help. The team turned out to be quite different from Pete's previous understanding of short-term mission teams. These people were older, at least in their 50's, and the many of them were retired. They were mostly from a large church in Texas and had gone on other missions together over a number of years. Unlike youth teams, these people knew the drill and there was not a lot of drama, so all Pete had to do was be available to translate for them, as needed.

The people in this group, being older and not as focused on themselves as a teenage mission team would be, took an interest in Pete and Carrie and asked about their ministry. When they heard about the Youth Center dream, they were intrigued. Having noticed the gangs of kids hanging out aimlessly on the streets, they could see the tremendous potential of such a project. One man in the group was retired from a career in commercial real estate, and wanted to check out the property Pete was considering. The whole team went along to look at the building and everyone was very impressed with it. Several of the men offered ideas about how to proceed with remodeling, and suggested considerations for keeping the business solvent once the Center was operating.

At the same time Pete was having virtual meetings with the elders and deacons of his home assembly who provided some very positive input, particularly regarding the spiritual direction of the project. They wanted to see the Center emphasize evangelistic outreach with a discipleship element worked in. The discipleship would focus on youth leaders from various churches who would be using the facility. They also cautioned Pete and Carrie about getting overloaded and burned out; having a good team of volunteers would be essential.

It was encouraging to Pete and Carrie to have so many people who were enthusiastic about developing the Youth Center, people who offered good ideas and advice. But the big question, the "elephant in the room" was how to fund such a dream. Surprisingly, the funding problem suddenly disappeared. As the departure date for the Texas Team was nearing, the group wanted to thank Pete by taking him and Carrie out for dinner. They told him to pick a really nice place and they even offered to pay for a babysitter for Olivia. Carrie knew just the place to choose—Fiesta Gourmet Restaurant.

And so it was, the night before the team returned to Texas, that Pete and Carrie found themselves enjoying a wonderful dinner in a restaurant that was renowned for class and atmosphere. As dessert was being served, one of the team members stood up and gave a little speech, thanking Pete for all the help he had been to them. Then he handed an envelope to Carrie, commenting that it contained a token of their appreciation for the fine missionary work that she and Pete were doing.

Carrie opened the envelope and gasped, as she read the note it contained. Wordlessly, and with tears in her eyes, she handed the note to Pete. He got choked up as he read the note, and it took a while before he could pull himself together and thank the group for their overwhelming kindness and generosity. They were offering to pay the full cost of the property that was being considered for the Youth Center! Pete could hardly believe it. The reality of the offer began to sink in as one of the men asked for Pete's bank account number and discussed how and when they would transfer funds.

With finances available, Pete signed the contract to buy the building. He calculated that it would take about two months to make the necessary improvements and move in. He soon learned that he was being way too optimistic. For starters, it took a full month for the purchase paperwork to be registered with the government. Once that hurdle was cleared, remodeling work began—and stopped almost immediately. The contractor Pete had hired to oversee the work found numerous code violations from work done in the past. He told Pete that the simplest thing to do was to "grandfather in" the sloppy work, correcting things as he went along. He admitted that these corrections would legally require updated licenses and redrawn architectural plans, but the simplest way to handle it would merely require some money changing hands.

Pete was shocked. His contractor, a Christian, was suggesting that they bribe their way around difficulties. Pete insisted on doing things legally and honorably, although it irked him that he was basically paying fines because of shortcuts in the past. It took extra time, and money, but Pete's conscience was clear. The work went on smoothly for a while, but eventually there were requirements that seemed impossible to meet legally. Jaime, the lawyer, searched for a reasonable solution and eventually told Pete they were at a dead end and the only way to get the job done was to go ahead without the required paperwork, and then pay a fine for not having the proper documents ahead of time.

With all these memories surfacing in his mind, Pete didn't notice that he was now at the front of the line at Sunarp. The guy behind him tapped Pete on the shoulder and motioned for him to move up to the counter. Quickly stepping up, Pete spread out all the documents for the official to consider. Everything seemed to be in order, so Pete was allowed to insert the paperwork into the wheels of bureaucracy. The official told him to check back in a couple of days before going on to the local authorities.

Leaving the Sunarp office, Pete looked at his watch and decided he had time to stop by the construction site on his way home. The place was looking good and was almost ready for final inspection of the remodeling work; hopefully, the municipal officials would get to it soon. Then a safety inspection would be required for the restaurant license. This included sanitary standards for the kitchen, fire extinguishers and clearly marked exits. Soon after all that transpired, they would be ready for their grand opening!

It was probably a blessing that the construction work took as long as it did. This gave Pete and Carrie time to think through the ministry side of the project. Pete had focused on getting a number of churches to commit to participating in the Youth Center. When he explained the concept there was initial excitement, but he found he had to share the vision a number of times at each church, with the leadership and then with the whole congregation before anyone would make a commitment. He ended up visiting each church three or more times to discuss the same information each time.

As people came on board with the project, Carrie began organizing training sessions for volunteers who would be helping in various ways. She was happy to have so many eager volunteers, more than she really needed. However, as time went on she began to sense some discontent. It turned out that this was the reason for Monica's visit this afternoon.

Monica and Pete arrived at almost the same time. Carrie had just put Olivia down for her late-afternoon nap, and then set out a plate of cookies and some cold drinks. Sitting around the kitchen table, Monica filled in Pete and Carrie on the unhappiness among the prospective Youth Center volunteers. Actually, it wasn't just unhappiness; feelings ranged from disappointment to anger to a sense of betrayal. Somehow, "volunteer" did not translate into Spanish with the same connotations that Carrie had in mind. Monica had heard more than one person say, "If the gringos have so much money to buy a building, why can't they pay people to work at the Center?"

Hearing Monica's news, Pete and Carrie were shocked and disappointed. They had been thinking that volunteering at the Youth Center would be a great opportunity for people to serve the Lord, and develop ministry skills. How sad to realize that some of their friends saw the project as simply a way to earn a little extra income.

After Monica left, Pete and Carrie talked over the situation long into the night. The problem was that a one-time gift to start a ministry was no guarantee that they could pay wages. Maintaining a paid staff would likely mean they would have to charge more for their service, which could discourage the evangelistic purpose. The kids they hoped to serve would certainly not be able to pay enough to cover the cost of running the place. If they tried to run the center with some volunteers and some paid staff, that could lead to all sorts of problems and hurt feelings. The thought of paying employees made Pete groan—he was savvy enough now to know that paying workers meant more paperwork and standing in lines.

Observations

What does it take for a project to really be ministry? When a missionary develops a project, he will see it as an avenue for ministry. A youth center is a means of reaching young people; a clinic is a way to serve people by caring for physical needs; a school might be started to give underprivileged kids a chance in life. In each case, the project is designed to minister to felt needs as a way of connecting with people on a spiritual or ministry level. Projects tend to be attractive; they are tangible and make good missionary reports, while ministry in a pure form is often not very exciting. Missionaries can be drawn to a project simply for the activity. It is an accomplishment; you have something to show for your time and effort. When developing a project, it is important to have the right spiritual motivation and clarity of purpose. A good project will enhance ministry rather than taking time and energy away from it. Keeping a balance between the social/physical need and the spiritual need is key.

When starting a project, a missionary may see the immediate need, but not the long-term picture. Ministry projects have a tendency to grow. Given enough time, the preschool develops into a K-12 establishment and the humble clinic becomes a hospital offering all kinds of advanced treatment. What happens when the missionary who started the work retires or dies? Will others be ready and willing to take over his work and carry it on?

Somehow, starting a ministry has much more appeal than picking up where someone else left off. Funding could be a serious consideration if a young missionary were to take over a ministry begun by a well-established worker who had, over the years, developed a strong group of supporters for his project. The new missionary might be hard pressed to provide the funding the ministry requires.

Money matters can cause problems in many ways, as Pete and Carrie discovered. The prevalence of bribery in business and legal matters creates serious headaches for the missionary whose Christian culture is strongly against this way of "greasing the wheels". Some have solved the issue by distinguishing between a bribe that is given and one that is mandated. The missionary who would never offer a bribe might be willing to pay one that is being demanded. In some situations, a bribe might be seen more as a tip, being given to someone whose wages are not sufficient for the job he is doing.

Bribes have a corrupting influence, and the missionary must be wary. I have come up with a policy for my own use. Bribing officials in the area where I live would destroy my local reputation, so I studiously avoid stooping to do anything of that nature. However, when I am traveling far from home and get into a situation where a policeman or some other authority is expecting a bribe, I would be more flexible. At that point, I would weigh the options and do whatever was needed to get out of trouble and back on the road.

How judgmental should we as missionaries be regarding our local brothers' business practices? Two areas where the true nature of sin comes out in a believer are soccer and money. In both areas the competitive need to win brings true character to light. As a missionary you can often observe it in one way or another. A certain brother comes late to church, wanting to keep his business open as long as possible. Not quite a sin, but an indication of misplaced priorities. In a situation like this I like to use my relationship with the brother as a platform for spiritual advice. Sometimes I need to get my hands dirty helping him close his business earlier. Even doing that, I know change will be a process, and probably a slow process at that.

In the last part of the story, we see money being a problem for ministry. There are so many variations on this theme, of locals looking to the missionary eagerly, but their interest is in the money you have access to. Anything from people knocking on your door for a handout, to "volunteering" in ministry—for money. Money damages relations and reputations so quickly. I've made a rule for myself never to lend money to a believer, but to give it, if I have it. Good advice I was given was to set aside a giving allotment each month so I could legitimately say, "I'm out of funds right now." It is a hard balance to strike because as a missionary you don't want to harden your heart to real needs. But sometimes if you give freely you will end up with a hard heart because of the betrayals you experience. So, money is a difficult thing to manage in ministry. One surprising thing is that often believers want the missionary to handle the money because they trust his integrity.

Questions

1. Is it possible for a missionary's project to not be a ministry? Can you think of any examples?

2. How can a missionary enable his ministry project to continue if he has to leave the field? Is it reasonable to expect others to take over a project that they did not initiate?

3. In many cultures the missionary will be perceived to be on a higher economic level than most people. What are some of the problems and misunderstandings that might result?

4. Bribes are normal in many parts of the world. How would you develop your own personal response?

13

When it Rains it Pours

Pete woke up for the second morning in a row in his pick-up truck, on the side of the road somewhere below Cajamarca. He realized it was silence that woke him; the diesel truck that had been rumbling for hours had gone quiet. *"Probably out of fuel,"* Pete thought. He was certain the big truck had not moved. Nobody had moved for something like thirty hours. Pete knew there were twenty-seven vehicles ahead of him, and probably that many more behind him, farther up the road. No up-hill traffic had come by—another indication that the highway was still blocked by people protesting the environmental degradation at Yanacocha, the huge, open pit gold mine located a mere 30 kilometers from Cajamarca.

Yesterday afternoon and the evening before that Pete had walked down to the line of scrimmage to seek information about when the road might reopen. He didn't learn anything useful. Rumors were easy to find and even start, if you wanted to, but real information was scarce.

Pete opened the door of the truck and eased out, shutting the door quietly so as not to wake Eber who was sleeping on the back seat of the double cab pickup. The eastern sky was just beginning to brighten above the mountains, and a few birds were chirping their morning songs. The air was cool and crisp. In other circumstances, Pete would have enjoyed the location, so much more scenic than the flat, barren land around Chiclayo. Looking to the west, he could see hillsides marked off into patches of pasture and farmland. The valleys, hidden by the hills, contained small settlements, usually just a collection of houses strung along both sides of the road. This early hour was a good chance for Pete to stretch his legs. He walked up hill a hundred meters or so to a place where the road looped around a gulley that was heavily overgrown. The shrubbery offered a somewhat private place to answer the call of nature, and Pete hoped no one else had gotten there ahead of him.

Walking back to the truck, Pete checked his cell phone, more or less out of habit. He knew there was no service here on his Claro plan, and besides that, the phone was about to die, even though he had it set on airplane mode to save the battery. When he got to the truck, Eber was sitting up, yawning and rubbing sleepy eyes. He looked like he had not slept very well. Pete was thankful to have Eber with him, which allowed him to leave the truck when he needed to, without worrying about stuff in the back being stolen.

The hardest part of this whole mess for Pete was being out of touch with Carrie. The last time they had talked was three days ago. At that time she told him that Olivia seemed to be coming down with the same bug Carrie had a week earlier. He felt terrible, not being there when his family needed him, but there was nothing he could do right now except wait and pray for the waiting to end.

Just over a week ago the trip had started off optimistically, with Pete taking seven kids from the youth group to a camp in the hills near Cajamarca. Organized by a church in town, the camp was held at a "fundo" (cattle ranch). Pete was the invited speaker, with an assigned topic for the week, "Facing Your Giants". He redirected the topic a bit, choosing to look at the world's influence on young college students. Not surprisingly given the location, the camp was pretty rustic with a makeshift kitchen under a barn roof, and tents to sleep in. Evenings were chilly and some of the kids from the coast did not bring adequate bedding. Surviving was part of the fun: bonfires warded off the cold and packing tight in the tents helped keep everyone warm enough.

The seven from Chiclayo had managed to scrape up money to pay half their camp fees, and Pete chipped in the rest, including free transportation in his truck. The free ride to camp was easy, but the trip back had gotten tricky. On their return from camp, they stopped at a gas station near Cajamarca where they heard rumors of an indigenous strike against the mines in the region. Pete noticed lots of vehicles heading out of town, trying to get away from whatever trouble might be brewing. Joining them with a full tank of gas and some fervent prayer, Pete put pedal to the metal, hoping to avoid getting stuck in the middle of nowhere.

Heading down the mountain, they ended up being part of a convoy of vehicles. Several times they passed groups of people dressed in traditional Andean clothing, chanting and marching along the road, but not impeding traffic. Glancing in the rear-view mirror, Pete was amused to see the three kids who were riding in the back of the truck filming the scene with their cell phones. He thought they looked like tourists.

Coming around one of the many hairpin bends in the road, Pete saw a line of cars and trucks stopped in front of him. Easing in behind a flatbed truck on the edge of the road, Pete turned off the engine and waited. Twenty minutes went by and several of the kids decided to check out the situation. They came back with news that this was, indeed, a blockade and it would probably not be lifted for hours or maybe days. They had heard that another blockade had formed a couple of kilometers behind them, so there was no point in trying to go back to Cajamarca.

By late morning the kids were getting antsy and were running out of snacks. Six of them decided to head out, leaving Pete and Eber with the truck. They figured they could walk cross-country to get around the blockade, and then try to hitch a ride when they got back to the road farther down. They left just after noon and hadn't been heard from since. Pete hoped their plan had worked and they had gotten back to civilization, no worse for the wear.

The blockade was unfortunate, but a fact of life in Peru. Such events were common, especially in the mountains. This particular blockade probably had something to do with Andean tribal groups wanting more money from the mining companies under the guise of protecting the environment which they believed the evil trans-national corporations were ruining. No doubt, there was some truth to the claims, and the mining company may have been reneging on previous agreements. The government usually got involved when things got bad enough, and a blockade was a good way to get attention from the authorities.

As the day warmed up some vendors walked along the road, selling snacks to people in the stranded caravan. Pete was wishing for some Dr. Pepper about now, but that was not on the limited menu. He and Eber were surviving, so far, on potato chips, crackers and some dried fruit. They really needed something to drink. Unfortunately, most of the vendors were offering home-made fruit drinks which they sold in plastic bags equipped with straws. Pete was leery of this kind of hydration, suspecting that the water was unfiltered, but Eber was thirsty enough to take a chance. A second problem was that Pete was almost out of money. He was down to his last 100 Soles, having given the rest of his cash to the six youths, hoping they could eventually get home by bus.

Around noon the distinctive whop-whop-whop sound of a helicopter gave everyone some hope that the military had arrived and would sort things out shortly. An hour later engines started, and the column of vehicles began rolling slowly down the hill. When they got to the site of the blockade, Pete and Eber noted police or military in riot gear holding back the remaining protesters and clearing the road. The fires that had been lit overnight had seared the pavement in places, but most of the boulders had been cleared off to the side. Beyond the blockade location there was no on-coming traffic for about five kilometers, until the point where another blockade was being cleared to allow traffic to start moving up toward Cajamarca.

It was almost 2:30 when traffic picked up to normal speed; Pete and Eber were thanking the Lord that they were finally on their way home. They stopped at large gas station near Ciudad de Dios where Pete was able to pay with his credit card. Besides fuel and much-needed food and drinks, he also bought a 12 volt USB adapter to charge his dead phone. Once the phone was revived, Pete was able to call Carrie to tell her where he was and when he would be home.

Carrie was relieved to hear Pete's voice, though she had already heard bits and pieces of the adventure from the six kids who managed to get into town the previous day. In addition to her concern about Pete, she had also dealt with a frightening situation with Olivia. The baby had been feeling miserable for several days, but Monday morning she seemed much worse. Carrie phoned for an appointment with the pediatrician at the clinic where Olivia was born. Monday was the doctor's day off, and Carrie was told to bring her daughter in first thing on Tuesday.

Needing help sooner than that, Carrie phoned her friend, Monica, who offered to go with her to the emergency room at the hospital. The situation there appeared chaotic to Carrie. The patients had no privacy; they were lying on rows of cots in a large room. Most of them were hooked up to IV bags with family members holding the bags aloft, as normal IV stands seemed to be in short supply. The noise was incredible, with patients moaning and anxious family members trying to get the attention of the one ER doctor who was on duty. There were no nurses in sight; Monica told Carrie that family members were supposed to do the basic care which included getting food for the patients and taking them to the bathroom as well as getting supplies from the pharmacy—if and when they could get a prescription from the overworked doctor.

Carrie recoiled at the idea of having her baby cared for in this environment, so Monica suggested going to the pharmacy for Tylenol. The pharmacist, a kindly middle-aged woman, administered the first dose and told Carrie to take Olivia home and give her frequent sponge-baths to help bring her temperature down. Hopefully, this treatment would keep the fever from spiking and sending Olivia into convulsions—an ominous thought for Carrie. Thankfully, the combination of Tylenol and sponge-baths helped, but neither Carrie nor Olivia got much sleep that night.

Tuesday morning Carrie was at the clinic when it opened, and the pediatrician was able to see Olivia right away. He ordered some lab tests and told Carrie that she could leave Olivia at the clinic overnight if she wanted to. Of course, she did not want to leave her baby for a minute. Since it would take a while to get the lab results, Carrie and Olivia were sent home and told to return in mid-afternoon. When they went back the doctor handed Carrie a prescription for an antibiotic and assured her that within a day or two Olivia would be feeling better. That turned out to be the case. In fact, by the time Pete finally made it home, Olivia was sound asleep and did not appear feverish.

It was after dark when Pete arrived. He had stopped at the church to drop off the luggage that had been left in his truck. Then he took Eber home, and Eber said he would phone the rest of the youth to tell them where to find their stuff. Both Pete and Carrie were dead tired and Carrie, especially, was frazzled, but they stayed up late, telling each other all that had happened in the days they had been apart. They were thankful to be back together again, and more than thankful that baby Olivia was on the mend.

Observations

The multitude of panic situations you can run into on the mission field would never fit in one book. This story is not the worst I could think of, and some stories I have heard were much, much worse. The problem with writing a fiction story is that it has to be believable—and some of the stories I know would be hard for most people to believe. As my dad said after an extremely crazy ordeal, "I can't tell anyone because nobody would believe me anyway."

Missionaries, being for the most part intelligent people, exhibit a fair bit of caution when dealing with difficult situations and are good at asking themselves, "What if???" As a result, they pack along extra medicine, money, fuel, spare parts, sat phones and food when they travel, since it is often when you are away from home that things get exciting. But life at home can also be stressful when you find yourself dealing with chronic problems. Missionaries have a tendency, when they spot a problem, to say "Let's fix it." They come from a culture where fixing things is the norm and people are always looking for ways to make life easier or better. It can be very frustrating to be living in a culture where people don't fix things, they just put up with inconveniences and discomfort. Many examples come to mind: electrical wiring, water supply, bathrooms, road maintenance, leaky roofs, hygiene, and on and on. Having said this, I should add that the nationals are not incompetent to fix their own problems, but their cultural values often lie elsewhere.

A good way to cope with the mishaps of living overseas is to think of life as an adventure. It can be a game-changer for a team coming for a week or two when you present this perspective to them. The volume of whining goes down and they can embrace some of the hardship in a new way. It is more difficult to adopt this perspective for the long haul and requires a deliberate mind-set of accepting the reality of your adopted culture. It is important to seek out and appreciate the virtues of that culture. If you don't, the frustrations will just get to you. I have known missionaries who went home when the adventure wore off and they were overwhelmed with the little grievances of daily life.

A lot can be said for being pro-active and finding ways to make life more pleasant or at least tolerable. The natives probably won't be offended if the missionary wants to have some sort of bathroom accommodation (though they may laugh behind his back). When I visited an indigenous tribal group I was surprised to learn that they had a bathroom (outhouse) for guests. I asked my missionary host if such a facility was normal in that part of the jungle. He explained that an earlier missionary, a woman, had insisted on having some privacy for that part of life. She had a hole dug—she brought in a post hole digger to speed up the work—with boards to stand on and some sort of privacy fence around the installation. No one else in the village used the missionary's outhouse; the locals knew that it was better to spread out their "offerings" rather than collect them in one place where the smell would get pretty ripe. For visitors from the outside world, it seems like the smell is an okay tradeoff for being able to have a little privacy.

We can't always improve situations for our comfort and convenience, but—thankfully—God has created people with the ability to adapt. Things that seem intolerable at first can eventually appear normal as our expectations mutate. There is a well-known joke about a missionary who discovers a fly in his soup. The first term missionary throws out the whole bowl of soup. The second term missionary strains out the fly. The third term missionary doesn't even notice that there is a fly in his soup.

Some of the most aggravating frustrations are the simple ones—the neighbor's dog that barks all night, or the people down the street who have a loud party every weekend, or the endless waiting in line at the bank. Things like this are beyond fixing; calling the police about neighbors disturbing the peace is not culturally acceptable. Waiting in a long line at the bank or some government office is a fact of life and complaining will not change things, except to give you an ulcer, maybe.

Just as this is being written the Covid-19 virus has struck as a world-wide pandemic. It is a problem here at home as well as in other parts of the world. There is an extra layer of complication for a missionary overseas, trying desperately to find a flight to get home. Meanwhile, other missionaries find themselves "stranded in the States" and not allowed to return to their place of service. As with any traumatic situation, our answer is going to be prayer and faith in God's providence. In addition, we will plan, save resources, and think of alternatives. In recent years many mission organizations have retained the services of security specialists to assess dangerous situations and help missionaries plan for extreme situations. But that is just the problem: no one saw Covid-19 coming, and anyway—how do you plan for a pandemic? The world tries to solve problems by throwing money at them. Our response should be first to pray and then be as careful and daring as God will allow us to be. It is, after all, an adventure.

Questions

1. Life will sometimes throw at us situations that we would never anticipate. Is it possible to prepare for such things? How would you do it?

2. If you can solve a problem by "throwing money at it", is this necessarily a bad solution? What might you be missing if you take this path?

3. Some people enjoy "living on the edge" while others tend to be over cautious and avoid risk. Is either style more spiritual than the other?

How should a missionary seek to honor the Lord in his approach to possibly dangerous situations?

4. How important is it to have a good attitude in bad circumstances? How can you develop such an attitude?

14

Where the Road Forks

Pete's mind was buzzing as he closed down his laptop after a one-hour conversation with Pastor Mike of Friendship Community Church. He was really surprised to get this call, as he didn't know Pastor Mike very well. However, Friendship Community Church had recently begun sending some financial support to him and Carrie. Pete figured it was due to the fact that a couple of families from his home assembly had moved to FCC so that their kids could be part of the church's top-notch youth program.

After some casual conversation, Pastor Mike had asked how things were going at the Christian Youth Center in Chiclayo and assured Pete that their missions pastor and committee regularly prayed for them and the Youth Center. Then he moved on to the reason for his call. He was very impressed with the youth outreach Pete and Carrie were doing and he wanted to invite them to help his church initiate something similar in their multi-ethnic community in California. Pastor Mike explained that, although they had a great youth group in the church, nothing was being done for the hordes of un-churched kids, particularly the immigrants in the area. With Pete and Carrie's experience in running a Youth Center which attracted kids from all segments of society, Pastor Mike thought they would be ideal to get something of the sort up and running in FCC's neighborhood. Concerning the time frame, what he was envisioning could involve them for a few years, or maybe it could be a permanent move.

Jotting some notes about the conversation, Pete was wishing Carrie had been home when Pastor Mike called. It would be hard to convey the whole conversation to her. Just after lunch Carrie had gone shopping, taking Olivia with her. After she got home, he would need to go to the Youth Center to supervise the set-up for this evening's activities. He figured he wouldn't have a good chance to discuss Pastor Mike's proposal with Carrie until sometime after dinner.

This call, coming out of the blue, certainly gave him a lot to think about. Up until now he had never imagined a change in ministry. Considering the possibility, Pete could see some advantages for the family. Carrie was well into her second pregnancy and they might need to find a bigger house after the baby's arrival. Their current house was barely adequate, and there was little space for Olivia to play outdoors. They had a tiny courtyard in back— actually, it was supposed to be a place to hang laundry to dry. Recently Pete had built a sandbox in one corner, and Olivia was thrilled with it. Almost every morning she woke up singing, "Sandbox! Sandbox!" Pete enjoyed being able to make her happy. The sandbox was great for right now, but kids grow up so fast. Someday she would be big enough for a bike and he looked forward to teaching her how to ride a two-wheeler. But—where could she ride a bike in this neighborhood? He wished he could give her a big back yard with some trees like he had when he was a kid.

As for the pregnancy, Carrie and Pete had on-going discussions as to where the next child should be born. Things had gone smoothly with Olivia's birth, but what if there was a difficult delivery? Various experiences they had had with the medical system were sobering. Surprisingly, it was Carrie who was leaning toward staying in Peru for the baby's birth, while Pete had reservations. They didn't have a real argument going on, just periodic discussions. As a result, they had not bought airline tickets, but Pete had set some money aside just to keep the options open.

Before Pete could continue pondering the possibilities brought up by Pastor Mike's call, his cell phone rang. It was Amber, the intern who had joined them a few months ago and had become a valuable co-worker at the Youth Center. Amber called to remind him of various food items needed for the snack bar, and also reported a serious leak problem with the kitchen sink. Pete told her he would do the shopping and try to get over to the Center by three o'clock. The sink would really complicate matters. The Center was scheduled to open at five o'clock, and that didn't leave a lot of time to work on the sink. Pete had learned that plumbing problems always turn out much more complicated and time-consuming than they should be.

As he tried to imagine what it might take to repair the leak, Pete rummaged through his tool collection and picked out the most useful items. Thinking that this would be a good opportunity to install a splitter in the line to add a fill hose for the large coffee maker, he made a mental list of parts he would need to pick up at the hardware store. He wondered if he would actually be able to pull off everything he was hoping to do.

As he packed up all his equipment, Pete heard Carrie outside, rummaging through her purse to find the front door key. She had already unlocked the wrought iron gate on the street and hauled the stroller into their miniscule garden. The space between the gate and the front door was just over one meter, meaning that she had to turn the stroller sideways to shut the gate and then squeeze around it to the front door. Somewhere in all that she had misplaced her keys, and she was getting frantic by the time Pete opened the door.

Olivia squealed with delight at seeing her daddy, and with a mischievous smile pulled out the keys from somewhere in her stroller. Carrie snatched the keys, saying, "Olivia! That was naughty!" Pete responded by picking up the toddler and holding her over his head, laughing. Now Carrie lit into Pete, telling him not to reward Olivia's bad behavior by laughing.

Still laughing, Pete replied, "But Honey—didn't you hear what she was saying? She said, 'Key! Llave! Our baby is bilingual!'"

Carrie had to laugh, too. This would be something to write in Olivia's Baby Book. Pete set the little girl down and maneuvered the stroller into the house. He helped Carrie unload her purchases while giving her a quick summary of Pastor Mike's call. They would definitely need to talk when he got home.

In an effort to save time, Pete chose to go to Sodimac (a home and garden center) for the plumbing parts—more expensive than the neighborhood hardware store, but it had the advantage of being located next to Tottus (a Peruvian Walmart) where he could pick up all the food items on Amber's list. An added attraction was the safe parking lot where he could leave his truck while he shopped.

Amber was relieved when Pete showed up shortly after three o'clock. She and Silvia, a girl from church who volunteered at the Youth Center, unloaded the supplies while Pete spread out his tools near the sink. When Amber phoned earlier Pete had told her how to turn off the water. Unfortunately, there was still a little residual pressure in the line and Pete got a small shower when he succeeded in wresting off the old faucet— which came apart in his hands. Unlike plumbing in the US where code was followed and new systems were continually more convenient, Peru required re-engineering every single time. Pete scraped and cleaned rust from the galvanized steel pipe coming out of the tiled wall. He needed to clean the threads enough to avoid cross-threading on the plastic pipes he would add. Peru had transitioned into glue and slide-on plastic joints. It was easy to put together a system with PVC but required some thinking ahead if you wanted to do maintenance in the future. Thankfully, he had brought a roll of Teflon tape to eliminate leaks.

Pete thought it was kind of ironic that when they were considering buying the building one of the attractive features was the kitchen with plumbing already installed. And now he was finding that the plumbing was substandard, and he could see that he would probably be making more repairs and upgrades in the future. Pete used screw-on clamps to attach the new water line to the tiles above the counter. Where the line ended near the big coffee maker, he installed a faucet. He had bought a countertop bowl but would have to plumb in a drain another day. In the meantime, he warned the girls—don't turn on this faucet! Amber, with Silvia's help, wrote a warning message in her best Spanish and taped it to the wall.

As Pete prepared to thread in the new faucet over the old sink, his phone rang. He continued to wrap the Teflon tape around the fixture threads as he balanced the phone on his shoulder. The call was from Pepe, one of the local pastors who had taken up the challenge of starting a church for Venezuelan migrants. He was finding it difficult to develop any real community among the group as there were only a couple of families who were stable enough to attend regularly. The other Venezuelans who came were shifting from job to job and often ended up moving away after a couple of months. Pete tried to help Pepe by preaching at his church occasionally.

A recent development that seemed to have promise was a Bible study Pete had begun with Pepe and several other pastors and elders. These men were serious about serving the Lord, but most had had very little training. Pete had worked hard, putting together a sort of mini-Bible school with homework and well-prepared lecture material. He liked to think of it as continuing on-the-job training for pastors. Pepe was calling to ask if a new friend could join their group. The man in question was a Venezuelan pastor who would likely move on soon, Pete suspected. However, Pete didn't feel he could turn down someone who apparently wanted and needed training.

By the time he got off the phone Pete had succeeded in threading the new faucet and was ready to turn on the water. Thankfully, a pressure test did not reveal any leaks. Pete picked up his tools while Amber and Silvia cleaned the counter with sanitizer and re-mopped the floor. Amber unlocked the front door and kids began to stream in. The youth group that was going to perform tonight showed up after a while, lugging in their instruments and some extra props. It was really too late for a practice session, but that's what they did while other kids lined up for food. Pete wished they could have practiced earlier, but he reminded himself that this is how it goes in Peru.

After a number of conversations that took a lot of time, Pete was on his way home. Carrie had dinner ready to serve and Olivia was in her highchair. As he came in the door she shouted, "Daddy! Food!" By the time they finished eating, it was almost time for Olivia's bedtime ritual, which seemed to get longer every week. She didn't have a very big vocabulary, but she managed to let them know that she needed one more song or one more story, or a drink of water. Pete always enjoyed humoring her, but finally Carrie had had enough. She scooped up a very tired little girl and carried her off to bed, after asking Pete to put on the kettle for tea.

When Carrie returned, Pete was pouring boiling water into the teapot after adding several decaf tea bags. He had searched around and found their stash of chocolate chip cookies. With the cookies on a plate and two mugs of steaming tea, he joined Carrie at the table. "Okay, Pete," Carrie opened the conversation, "what's the story about the call with Pastor Mike?"

Observations

This story gives us the opportunity to explore the question of changing direction on the mission field. When an interesting new opportunity presents itself, most people will spend considerable time thinking through the possibilities. Sometimes it will be obvious that the new venture is a bad idea, but often something new looks very attractive. We know the problems and frustrations of our current situation, but another option may seem exciting and perfect. Realistically, we have to realize that there will be problems wherever you go and some of the problems are the ones you bring along with you. It is a good idea to "do the math" when considering a major change: make lists of values—what is gained by staying where you are, and what is gained by moving to a different work. Things to consider include ministry potential—how many people can you reach in your present work or in the new venture? What about personal gifting—will your gifts fit in better somewhere other than where you are now? What can you contribute to a project? Can you get along with the organizational structure and the other people involved in the work?

An argument for staying was implied in the story. Pete had a collection of responsibilities that were critical, particularly with the Youth Center and the mini-Bible school he had started. If he were to leave, what would happen to these ministries? Jumping around from one thing to another may give you experiences but does not lead to lasting fruit. Ministries are built around people and these relationships require cultivation and investment in order to make a long-term impact. There should always be the goal of training others to take your place, but there is also the aspect of leading by example and not forcing transitions to occur.

I have had the experience (privilege or misfortune) of leaving the mission field at least once. My great concern, as the transition loomed, was to leave things well established. I knew that no one person was going to replace me, but I had reason to hope that several whom I had trained would step in and take up various responsibilities. I think it was good for them to be "pushed out of the nest", so to speak. At the time, some of my principles were theoretical, but years later I can see how God was able to use my departure for greater growth among others.

In the first few years of this century a new mission theory developed and was taken up enthusiastically by various missionary organizations. The theory related to the amount of time a missionary should take to finish up and move on. A short cycle missions model was being promoted, suggesting that, like the apostle Paul, you should get in and get out in four years or so. If you didn't, you were an incompetent missionary, just marching in place and trying to maintain your position in the country. This theory reflected very negatively on those who chose to stay long-term in one location, which had been quite the normal procedure until then. I remember discussing this idea at length with some proponents, and not being convinced of the practicality of this idealism.

Along the same line, a characteristic that has rocked missions more recently is the attitude and expectations of the younger generation. There is a reluctance to commitment of any kind, coupled with an eagerness for adventure and exciting experiences. On the mission field this leads to quick turnover of workers with half-baked ministries left in their wake.

Questions

1. The short-cycle mission theory is based on the Apostle Paul's example. What are some factors that worked in Paul's favor, but may not be available in many of today's mission fields?

2. What are some indicators that a missionary has accomplished his task and should move on?

3. What role should the "sending team" (church elders or mission board leaders) play in helping the missionary decide if he should leave, and how soon should they be consulted?

4. Should the "sending team" ever tell a missionary that he needs to leave the field? Why?

5. What might be the fall-out if a missionary changes directions frequently?

Jesse Mattix & Peggy Covert

Conclusion

One purpose for writing this book is to help people visualize that scary step of faith—the choice to become a missionary—and then explore some of the paths that can lead to overseas missionary work. But even before taking that first step, there are a number of hurdles that can discourage the prospective missionary. Two particular obstacles, often introduced by well-meaning people, are the *pedestal* and the *guilt trip*.

The pedestal refers to the idea of glorifying missionaries, particular those in the past who did heroic things and sometimes died as martyrs. Their stories are interesting and compelling, so it is not surprising that books have been written about them. Reading the biographies or hearing these historic figures lauded by preachers, a young person can get a skewed idea of what it takes to serve the Lord overseas. We should remember that for every one of these amazing individuals, there are probably hundreds of equally dedicated but ordinary workers who quietly served the Lord for long years, yet did not do anything spectacular, so nothing was written about them. While it is good to honor the heroes of the faith, leaders should be careful not to praise them to the extent that young people give up any hope of aspiring to such heights and conclude, "I guess I don't have what it takes to be a missionary."

The guilt trip is another trap that can keep people from considering missionary service. Unfortunately, it is sometimes missionaries themselves who introduce this obstacle, since they see the need so clearly and want to enlist future workers. Suggesting that everyone should be a missionary, or at least volunteer for missionary work, can lead people to avoid even thinking about whether the Lord is calling them to full-time overseas work.

In addition to these concerns is the idea of having a "call" to be a missionary. Testimonies of very dramatic calls can cause someone who is truly interested in full-time service to doubt his fitness for the job because of not having such an experience. So often, a "call" is a sum of little things, interest, opportunity, friends, prayers, events and a nudge in the right direction. Sometimes multiple generations in a family or even church groups (Moravians) are strongly led into missions and though that is statistically improbable, it is likely a result of cultivating hearts and minds.

The Bible puts the burden of going not on a personal call from God, but rather on needs in the field. 'I tell you, look up and see that the fields are already white for harvest!' (John 4:35 NASB)

And so, this book has been written, using fictional characters to show how someone might be led into missionary service in a way that is not too mysterious to contemplate. The paths that led Pete, Carrie and their friend Alex to go out in the Lord's work are among many possibilities available. We are blessed that in our time there are multiple small choices that can be made as trial steps into missions, compared to the early days of "modern misstons" when people boarded a sailing ship with the very real possibility of never coming home from some far-off field.

Another purpose in writing this book, particularly as a story, is to show the tricky situations that come up on the mission field. Cultural adaptation ranks high on the list of potential minefields. We grow up learning our own culture more or less by osmosis, not thinking about it, just accepting it as normal. Arriving in a new culture, the missionary will likely make plenty of mistakes, which can be costly in various ways. Sometimes the cost will be money to straighten out simple mistakes; fines may be levied, or bribes requested. More often it will cost you some pride in recognizing that your right way of doing something is not their right way of doing it. Apologies for social blunders are so common it becomes routine. Inconveniences and encroachments on your personal space or property are things you just have to smile at, or at least ignore as part of the cost of serving the Lord in a foreign culture.

Something else that is a cost for the missionary is separation from extended family and from your own family as your children grow up and go away for education. This separation is something to be counted on, expected, and appropriately planned for. Sometimes you are not there for the big events—the weddings, funerals, graduations, and other life events. This is part of the cost that needs to be counted when a person signs up for overseas service. I have sometimes heard the idealistic claim that missionaries go out to the field because they have such a compelling love for the people. To that idea I would warn that love for people wears thin pretty quick, so you need to bank on something deeper. What you sacrifice for, what you are willing to pay the cost for, is the love of the Lord Jesus Christ; nothing else will do.

Reading this book may—or may not—lead you toward the mission field. A more realistic hope is that you would have a commitment to missions regardless of your role and calling in God's work. You may be continuing with your secular job and serving in your local church, but can you understand a missionary better and pray for him with more understanding? Will you read his letters and understand some of what is written between the lines? Are you more aware of his needs and his family's needs when they return to the home country? Perhaps you will go to visit him, not just to do some missionary tourism but to encourage and help. Better yet, maybe you will be able to connect with the next generation, helping them discover something of what God can do through them as you help to build them up in the faith. In summary, I hope you will strengthen your commitment to "Love the Lord your God" and to love all that He is doing in the world.

About the Authors

Jesse Mattix has served as a missionary to Peru and Bolivia over the last 17 years. Along with his wife Janel they raised their two children, Fionna and Isaac on the field. Their primary mission was training young leaders with a one-year Bible School program.

Other ministries included business ventures, church planting, discipleship, bridge engineering and more. After 13 years they were invited to Peru to help start a similar Bible program in the northern jungle. Jesse has the added insight of having been born and raised on the mission field, enjoying this immensely.

Peggy Covert and her husband, Dan, have been part of the home team for a number of missionaries, encouraging and supporting them in various ways. Over the past 40 years they have had the privilege of visiting missionaries in twenty countries. Peggy has frequently written reports for a mission magazine. One of Dan and Peggy's joys has been the opportunity to lead children's classes at numerous missionary conferences.

Jesse Mattix & Peggy Covert

Jesse Mattix and Peggy Covert are available for interviews and personal appearances.
For more information contact us at info@advbooks.com

To purchase additional copies of these books, visit our bookstore at:
www.advbookstore.com

Advantage
BOOKS

Longwood, Florida, USA
"we bring dreams to life"™
www.advbookstore.com